THE HINDU CONCEPTION OF THE FUNCTIONS OF BREATH

THE HINDU CONCEPTION OF THE FUNCTIONS OF BREATH

A STUDY IN EARLY HINDU PSYCHO-PHYSICS

ARTHUR H. EWING

GYAN

Published by

Gyan Publishing House
5, Ansari Road
Daryaganj, New Delhi-110002
Phone: 011-47034999, 9811692060
E-mail: books@gyanbooks.com

Distribution Network
gyanbooks.com
India, USA, Canada, UK, Australia

ISBN: 978-93-6780-705-7 (PB)
First Published, 1901

2nd Impression 2024

Printed at: Gyan Press, Delhi.

THE HINDU CONCEPTION OF THE FUNCTIONS OF BREATH
Author: ARTHUR H. EWING

THE HINDU CONCEPTION OF THE FUNCTIONS OF BREATH

A STUDY IN EARLY HINDU PSYCHO-PHYSICS

ARTHUR H. EWING, M.A.

A DISSERTATION

Submitted to the Board of University Studies of the Johns Hopkins University for the Degree of Doctor of Philosophy.

1901

The Hindu Conception of the Functions of Breath.—A Study in Early Hindu Psycho-physics.—By Dr. ARTHUR H. EWING, Allahabad, India.

INTRODUCTORY AND FUNDAMENTAL.

THE Yajur-Veda, the Atharva-Veda, the Brāhmaṇas and the Sūtras contain frequent references to a number of vital breaths. These are expressed either by the plural of the word *prāṇa*, or by a series of words, formed by the combination of adverbial prefixes with the root √*an* "to breathe," viz.: *prāṇa*, *apāna*, *vyāna*, *udāna*, *samāna*, and *avāna*. These vital breaths or *prāṇas* are manipulated with especial frequency in connection with ritual practices. The exigencies of the ritual determine what and how many breaths shall be exploited. This exploitation of the *prāṇas* attains its most luxuriant form in connection with the building of the great Fire-altar (Agnikṣetra). The Fire-altar is conceived of under various forms. Sometimes its shape is supposed to be like a bird (cf. ÇB. Books vii.–x.); sometimes like a sacrificial animal (ÇB. viii. 1. 4. 3, etc.); sometimes like a human being (ÇB. iv. 1. 1. 1; vi. 1. 1. 5; vii. 4. 1. 23, etc.).

The living organism (*ātman*), thus assumed, cannot exist without vital breaths, and, accordingly, under various arrangements of name and number, they hold a large place in its construction. When names are given, the reference is to breathing processes, real, or analogically assumed. When numbers are given, the emphasis is either upon the location of a separate breath in the several parts of the body (ÇB. viii. 3. 4. 4, etc.), or upon either the psychical organs, or their activities, both organs and activities being called *prāṇas*.

This distinction between a plurality by names and a plurality by number is fundamental and divides the subject of the vital breaths into two well-defined spheres of investigation. The latter is the much more important of the two in their relation to Hindu thought. It not only directly introduces the question of the relation between the psychical *prāṇas* and the cosmico-divine concepts, Agni, Vāyu, etc.—thus involving the whole question of psycho-physical correlations; but it leads to the discussion of the various meanings of *prāṇa* in the singular—thus raising the problem of the relationship between *prāṇa* and the psychical and metaphysical concept, Atman. The former is formulaic, or largely so, and smacks of the ritual, and hence is less fruitful than might, at first sight, be anticipated.

At the same time, the series of names, whether representing observed and observable breath activities, or being mainly symbolic additions to an empiric starting-point, is worthy of careful investigation, because of the large place which these names hold in the literature, and because of the attempts at explanation which appear in the Upaniṣads.

PRĀṆA IN THE RIG-VEDA.

The propriety of making the Rig-Veda the starting-point in this discussion is self-evident. Its material, moreover, will be found to be fundamental to both divisions of the subject as above indicated, and, therefore calls for preliminary investigation.

Though the amount of material is comparatively meagre, yet the importance of the literature in which it is found, justifies a somewhat detailed statement which will contain all the uses both of the noun *prāṇa* and the verb $\sqrt{an}$.

The noun occurs but five times, viz.: i. 66. 1; iii. 53. 21; x. 59. 6; x. 90. 13; x. 189. 2. It is formed from the verbal root $\sqrt{an}$, "to breathe," by the addition of the prefix *pra*.

RV. i. 66. 1.

In this stanza *prāṇa* is one of the things with which fire (*agni*) is compared. It is said to be "like excellent riches, like the sun, like life (*āyus*), like one's own son."

The point to be noted here is the identification of "breath" and "life." The two words stand side by side without a connective. The accent of *áyus* shows it to be a noun. Even if, according to a recognized Vedic usage, we allow an adjectival force to *āyus* and translate by "living breath," there will be a clear hint of identification. In i. 48. 10, the derivative *prāṇana* stands side by side with *jīvana* in a line addressed to the Dawn, thus: "The very breath (and) life of all are in Thee, O joyous One, when Thou shinest forth." There is no connective between the words *prāṇana, jīvana*, and they may be translated "Breath, even life," "*viçvasya hi prāṇanaṁ jīvanaṁ tve*, etc." *Prāṇana* may indeed be taken as a causative adjective.

RV. iii. 53. 21.

Yam u dviṣmas tam u prāṇo jahātu, "Whomsoever we hate, let his breath leave him." This suggests the witchcraft practices which are especially characteristic of the Atharva-Veda. The identification of death and departing breath, as assumed here, is axiomatic and requires no remark.

RV. x. 59. 6.

Here *prāṇa* is sought by prayer, side by side with other parts and powers of the human organism, viz.: eye, mind (*manas*) and life-principle (*asu*).

RV. x. 90. 13.

This hymn is the famous Puruṣa-sūkta. In stanza 13, the wind (*Vāyu*) is said to have been produced from the breath of cosmic man. As the giant form of a primeval cosmic man undoubtedly took shape in the poet's thought by a projection of himself upon the universe, we are justified in interpreting each part and organ as though, at least in the first instance, the individual earthly man was referred to. *Prāṇa* is, therefore, the physical breath whose identity with wind is here assumed. The second half of the stanza runs, *mukhād indraç cā 'gniç ca prāṇād vāyur ajāyata.* These words not only express the axiomatic identification of *wind* and *breath*, to which countless references are made in Hindu literature; but the derivation of Agni from the mouth, whence issues the *warm* vital breath, which is also used in the production of fire, suggests the still more oft-recurring correlation of *agni* and *prāṇa*.

RV. x. 189. 2.

This stanza occurs in a hymn to Sūrya. The shooting forth of the rays is likened to the exhalation of animal breath.

Antaç carati rocanā 'sya prāṇād apānatī, "The shining one, breathing out (or off) from his breath moves about within." The third pāda adds, "The mighty one illumines the heaven." Whatever be the detailed interpretation and reference of these words, it is clear that *prāṇa* is here viewed simply as physical breath.

Verbal and Participial Forms of the Root $\sqrt{an}$.

These forms, whether from the simple root or the root compounded with prefixes, are of equal importance with the noun, and indeed, because of their variety, even more suggestive. There are two forms made from the simple root :

RV. x. 129. 2.

This is the important "*Nāsadāsīya*" theosophic hymn. The Vedic Imperfect *ānīt* is found in the second stanza thus :

Ānīd avātaṁ svadhayā tad ekaṁ, "That One, without wind, breathed by Its own will." This passage expresses by contrast the dependence of breath upon wind (*vāta*). That which differentiates the primitive Only from all else is the fact that It performed the act of breathing without having *wind* to start with.

RV. i. 164. 30.

Here the participle *anat* is used. The verse describes a "breathing swift-moving, living (*jīvam*), self-stirring One, who lies firm-fixed in the midst of our dwellings." Though Grassman rightly describes this line as obscure, and its connection with the context is not easy to make out, yet there seems no reason to doubt that the main reference is to the house-fire. The flaming up of fire seems to the poet's fancy like the breathing process of animal life.

We find three instances of $\sqrt{an}$ compounded with *pra*.

RV. x. 32. 8.

The form used is the imperfect *prāṇīt.* The line runs as follows: "Just now to-day he breathed"—*adyed u prāṇīt*—"he remembered those days (when) hidden, he sucked the bosom of his mother." The hymn is addressed to Indra. The connection of the stanzas is uncertain and the meaning obscure. Here probably the reference is to the fire which has been hidden in wood, which is produced by water. Sāyaṇa is doubtless right in thinking that the poet here speaks of the fire which has just been produced by the friction of the churning-sticks rubbed together. The word *prāṇīt* is doubly suggestive. (1) The breath of life is a fitting figure of the issuing forth of fire from wood, as, to the Hindu observer, it seems to do. (2) Breath was used along with the churning-sticks in the production of fire, and, therefore, to say that "Agni breathed" is an expression justified by the phenomenon.

RV. x. 125. 4.

Prāṇiti stands here side by side with verbs of seeing and hearing. The goddess Speech (Vāc) speaks in her own praise, "By me doth he who sees, breathes, and hears what is said, obtain (lit. 'eat') food." All breath movements are clearly included in the one word.

RV. x. 121. 3.

In this third stanza of the well-known Hiraṇyagarbha hymn, the participle *prāṇat* is used. It stands with the participle *nimiṣat*. Hiraṇyagarbha is declared to be the sole Ruler of all that moves (*jagat*) both the "breathers" and the "eye-closers," cf. AV. x. 8. 6 and xii. 1. 3 and 4. The distinction between the two classes of beings here mentioned, if there be a real distinction, is not clear. The gods are said to be *animiṣantaḥ*. Mitra is so called in RV. iii. 59, and vii. 60. Bṛhaspati is described as "*animiṣācārya*," "The teacher of the gods," cf. PW. "Breathers" may therefore include both earthly and heavenly beings, while "eye-closers" describe only the former. On the other hand, it is not impossible to understand by "breathers" heavenly beings who do not close their eyes, who "neither slumber nor sleep." The former of the two opinions is preferable, since *breathing* is the most salient phenomenon of all moving life.

In connection with these three examples of *pra* with √*an*, it is to be noted that the prefix adds nothing in the way of defining the direction of the breath movement. At most the difference between √*an* with *pra* and √*an* alone is one of intensity. Both forms cover breathing in general, without any hint of distinction between in-breathing and out-breathing.

√an with apa. RV. x. 189. 2.

The form used is the feminine of the present participle. The passage has already been discussed under *prāṇa*. The important words are *prāṇād apānatī*, which have been translated, "breathing out (or off) from his breath." The prefix *apa* has the force of "out," "off," or "away from." Here we have the sole Rig-Vedic basis of the noun form *apāna*.

√an with sam. RV. x. 55. 5.

This stanza contains the only instance of this compound in the Rig-Veda. The form used is the perfect. The theme under treatment is the moon. The context expresses the thought that the old moon swallows up the new one. "Behold the wisdom of the gods"—so runs the line—"to-day he died, yesterday he came to life"—*adyā mamāra sa hyaḥ sam āna.* The force of the prefix in such a connection is rather uncertain. PW. suggests both "aufathmen" and "zu Leben kommen." The latter seems preferable since it may be inferred from the literal meaning of the compound, viz.: "breathed together." Probably the force of the prefix is merely intensive and we might translate by the simple word "breathes;" for to breathe is to live and in contrast with *mamāra* means to come to life.

Summary of Results for the Rig-Veda.

(1) Including *prāṇana* with *prāṇa*, there are six passages where the noun is used. In three of them *prāṇa* signifies *breath in general*, cf. x. 59. 6; x. 90. 13 and x. 189. 2. In the three other passages it is put more or less definitely for *life*, cf. i. 48. 10; i. 66. 1 and iii. 53. 21.

(2) The prefix *pra* adds at most a slight intensive force to the root $\sqrt{an}$.

(3) The prefix *apa* has the force of "out" or "off" and its use in the single instance is of value in determining the meaning of *apāna*.

(4) The use of *sam* with $\sqrt{an}$ throws no light upon the meaning and use of *samāna*.

The Rig-Veda, therefore, shows, on the one hand, absolutely no indication of any attempt to specialize various breaths, and, on the other hand, furnishes no instance of the plural number of *prāṇa* and only those uses of the singular which are primitive and axiomatic.

CHAPTER I.

VIEWS OF TRANSLATORS AND SUMMARY OF MATERIAL.

A. Diverse and Varying Views of Leading Translators.

We take up first the Name series of vital breaths. The series of names is as follows: *prāṇa, apāna, vyāna, udāna,* and *samāna.* To these may be added the unique *avāna,* which appears but once, viz., in JB. Up.,[1] ii. 5. Apart from the challenge to investigation thrown out by such a series of names, the conflicting views of translators, notably as regards *prāṇa* and *apāna,* indicate that there is need for a careful survey of and inquiry into the whole material which the earlier literature supplies.

[1] Otherwise Talavakāra Upaniṣad-Brāhmaṇa.

The situation, as illustrated by the work of leading translators, is, briefly stated, as follows:[1]

(1) Haug, in his Āitareya Brāhmaṇa, is consistent. *Prāṇa* is given throughout as "air inhaled" and *apāna* as "air exhaled." One single textual slip must be noted. His text in iv. 14. 5, has *prāṇodānāu*, but he still translates as though it were *prāṇāpānāu*, or *prāṇa* and *apāna*.

(2) Böhtlingk also in his translation of the Bṛhadāraṇyaka Upaniṣad adheres to Einhauch and Aushauch for *prāṇa* and *apāna* with entire consistency.

(3) Bloomfield, in his "Hymns of the Atharva-Veda" (SBE., vol. xlii), is consistent throughout. He translates *prāṇa* by "in-breathing," and *apāṇa* by "out-breathing," whether they appear as separate words or in the copulative compound *prāṇāpānāu*. In only one instance (AV. xii. 3. 28) is there a variation made, and this is merely verbal, as for example when the compound is translated by the phrase "breaths of life."

(4) Griffith, in his translations of the Atharva-Veda and the Vājasaneyi-Saṁhitā of the White Yajur-Veda, generally makes the same distinction between *prāṇa* and *apāna* as that made by the translators already mentioned. "In-breath and out-breath;" "inhaling and exhaling;" "inspiration and expiration"—these are some of the forms of translation which he uses.

(5) Müller, in his translation of certain Upaniṣads (SBE. vols. i. and xv.), takes a different view. *Prāṇa* is rendered by "up-breathing" fifteen times; "breath that goes up," twice; "breath" twice, and "scent" three times. *Apāna*, on the other hand, appears as "down-breathing" twenty times; "breath that goes down," twice, and "off-breathing," once.

(6) Röer, in his translation of Upaniṣads (Bibl. Indica, vol. ii., pt. iii.) renders *prāṇa* by "vital air which goes forward," or by "breath;" and *apāna* by "vital air which goes downward or descends."

(7) Rajendra Lala Mitra, in his Chāndogya Upaniṣad, translates *prāṇa* and *apāna* in i. 3. 5 by "respiration" and "inspiration;" in other passages he merely transliterates the words.

(8) Cowell in Māitri Upaniṣad (Bibl. Indica, 1870) gives for *prāṇa* "air which goes upward," three times, and "respiration,"

---

[1] Add now: Caland, ZDMG. lv. 261 ff.; Böhtlingk, *ibid.* 518. [Note of correction.]

once; and for *apāna* "air which goes downward," three times, and "descending air," once.

Thus far we have found a measure of consistency in divergence of views. On the crucial question as to the meaning of *prāṇa* when contrasted with *apāna*, Haug, Böhtlingk, Bloomfield, and Griffith decide for "in-breathing," while Müller, Röer, Mitra, and Cowell think that the word means "out- or up-breathing."

(9) With Deussen, however, in his "Sechzig Upaniṣads des Veda," there enters what appears to be the greatest confusion. No attempt at translation is made except in five Upaniṣads, viz.: Ch. Up.; Bṛh. Ār. Up.; Kaṭh. Up.; Āit. Up., and Tāitt. Up. In all other cases where the words occur they are merely transliterated. A careful scrutiny of the material in the above-named Upaniṣads shows that the passages have been about equally divided between the two opposing lines of opinion. By including a few references in which the verbs $\sqrt{an}$ with *pra*, and $\sqrt{an}$ with *apa* are used, we find that in thirteen instances *prāṇa* and *apāna* are translated by "Aushauch" and "Einhauch," and in fourteen instances by "Einhauch" and "Aushauch." Of the five Upaniṣads mentioned above, four are represented in both lists. It is only fair to say just here that this divergence does not represent the inadvertence of hurried translation, since our author emphasizes his opinion in certain footnotes, while in his "Allgemeine Geschichte der Philosophie," vol. i. (a) pp. 248 ff. he defends the view that *prāṇa* sometimes means "Aushauch."

(10) However surprising the above results from Deussen, Eggeling, in his five volumes of the Çatapatha Brāhmaṇa (SBE., vols. xii., xxvi., xli., xlii., and xliv.), presents even greater variation in translating the terms under discussion. In order to understand the situation the additional breath-name *udāna* must be included in our review. In about forty passages *prāṇa* and *udāna* are translated as "out-breathing and in-breathing." In ÇB. i. 4. 3. 11 and 12, however, where *prāṇa*, *apāna*, and *udāna* occur, the first two are translated by "out-breathing and in-breathing," and *udāna* by "up-breathing." In many other places, also, the translation of *udāna* is "up-breathing." In the last volume of his work, which has recently issued from the press, viz., in 1900 (SBE., vol. xliv.), *udāna* is in every instance rendered by "up-breathing."

As to *prāṇa* and *apāna*, they appear in book i. as "out-breathing," and either "down-breathing" or "off-breathing." In books xi.–xiv. there is evidence of another insight and so *prāṇa* is represented either by "breath" or "out- (and in-) breathing," or "in-breathing;" while *apāna* appears everywhere as "off-breathing;" cf. also ix. 2. 1. 17, where we have a single instance of the rendering which prevails in the last four books, i. e., "in-breathing" and "out-breathing."

B. SUMMARY OF MATERIAL.

Prāṇa, Apāna, Vyāna, Udāna, and Samāna.

It will be a distinct gain to have before the mind as definite an idea as possible of the extent and distribution of the material which comes under what we may call the Prāṇa-Series, especially as only a small portion of it is to receive detailed treatment.

To this end the following summary of such material as is found in the Vedas, Upaniṣads, important Brāhmaṇas, and certain of the Sūtras, has been prepared.

I. Material in re the Prāṇa-Series in the White Yajur-Veda.

The Vājasaneya Saṁhitā contains the names of all the five members of the series. No attempt at an explanation of the various terms is made. The number and location of the references are as follows :

Prāṇāpānāu	Once.
Prāṇa and *apāna*	Twice.
Prāṇa, apāna, vyāna	Nine times.
Prāṇa, apāna, vyāna, udāna	Three times.
Prāṇa, apāna, vyāna, udāna, samāna	Once.
Prāṇa, vyāna, udāna	Twice.
Prāṇa, udāna, vyāna	Once.
Prāṇa, vyāna	Once.
Prāṇa, udāna	Once.
Prāṇas, vyāṇas (100 *prāṇas*, 1000 *vyānas* of Agni)	Once.

Note that *samāna* appears but once, and that *vyāna* surpasses *apāna* in frequency of use.

II. Material in re the Prāṇa-Series in the Atharva-Veda.

Prāṇāpānāu	Nineteen times.
Prāṇa and *apāna*	Seventeen times.
Prāṇas and *apānas*	Three times.

Prāṇa, vyāna .... Once.
Seven prāṇas, apānas, vyānas .... Once.
Prāṇa, apāna, vyāna .... Eleven times.
Prāṇāpānāu and *vyānodānāu* .... Twice.
Prāṇa, apāna, vyāna, samāna .... Once.
Vyāna .... Once.

Verbs and Participles.

The simple verb √*an* is used once. √*An* with *pra* is used as a verb thirteen times, and as a participle eight times. √*An* with *apa* appears twice as a verb and once as a participle. √*An* with *vi* is used once in its participial form, and √*an* with *ud* once as a finite verb.

Note that we have no instance in the AV. where the five names appear together.

Note also the large use of *prāṇa* and *apāna*, in comparison with their meagre use in VS.

III. Material in r e the Prāṇa-Series in the Çatapatha Brāhmaṇa.

Our résumé here includes the entire Brāhmaṇa with the exception of that part of book xiv. which is handled separately as the Bṛh. Ār. Upaniṣad. Eleven of the references which enter into the following count are quoted from the Vājasaneya Saṁhitā.

Prāṇodānāu .... Forty-one times.
Prāṇa, udāna, vyāna .... Fifteen times.
Prāṇa, apāna, vyāna .... Six times.
Prāṇa, vyāna, udāna .... Five times.
Prāṇa, apāna .... Seven times.
Prāṇa, apāna, vyāna, udāna .... Three times.
Prāṇa, apāna, udāna .... Twice.
Prāṇa, apāna, vyāna, udāna, samāna ..... Twice.
Prāṇa, vyāna, apāna, udāna, samāna ..... Once.
Prāṇa, udāna .... Four times.
Vyāna, udāna .... Once.
Prāṇa, vyāna .... Once.
Udāna .... Once.

IV. Material in r e the Prāṇa-Series in the Tāittirīya-Āraṇyaka.

The material from the Āraṇyaka given below does not claim to be exhaustive. What is here represented has been collected with the aid of Bloomfield's Concordance of the Mantras and Formulas of Hindu literature. This Concordance has been made available to the writer in MS. form. Inasmuch as the Prāṇa-Series is formulaic, it is probable that very little, if any, material has been omitted from the following list :

Prāṇa, apāna, vyāna, udāna, samāna ..... Nine times.
Prāṇa, vyāna, apāna .... Twice.
Prāṇa, apāna, vyāna .... Once.
Prāṇāpānāu .... Once.

V. Material in re the Prāṇa-Series in the Gopatha Brāhmaṇa.

This Brāhmaṇa contains both the Prāṇava and Gāyatrī Upaniṣads (i. 1. 16–30 ; 31–38). In the Upaniṣad material there is only one reference to the Prāṇa-Series ; hence we summarize here the entire Brāhmaṇa.

Prāṇapānāu .... Ten times.
Prāṇa, apāna, vyāna .... Three times.
Prāṇa, apāna, vyāna, samāna .... Once.
Seven prāṇas, apānas, vyānas .... Once.
Fifteen prāṇas, apānas, vyānas, samānas, udānas .... Once.
Seven prāṇas, apānas .... Once.
Prāṇa, udāna .... Once.
Prāṇāpānāu, samānavyānāu, udānarūpe .. Twice.

VI. Material in re the Prāṇa-Series in the Upaniṣads.

There is included in the following review the sixty Upaniṣads translated by Deussen, the Jāiminīya Brāhmaṇa Upaniṣad, and the Bhagavad Gītā. The whole is, for the purpose of the present summary, viewed as a unit. Many of the references here will be considered in detail later. Perhaps the most notable feature is the marked variation in the order in which the names appear. The uses of verbs and participles are omitted, as practically all instances are to be noted later.

Apāna .... Three times.
Prāṇāpānāu .... Seven times.
Prāṇa and *apāna* .... Seventeen times.
Prāṇa, apāna, vyāna .... Ten times.
Prāṇa, vyāna, apāna .... Twice.
Prāṇa, apāna, vyāna, samāna .... Twice.
Prāṇa, apāna, vyāna, samāna, avāna ... Twice.

Prāṇa, apāna, vyāna, samāna, avāna, udāna. Twice.
Prāṇa, apāna, vyāna, samāna, udāna ....Four times.
Prāṇa, apāna, vyāna, udāna, samāna.....Nine times.

(Three from Mahānārāyaṇa Up., i. e. TĀ., book X.)

Prāṇa, apāna, samāna, udāna, vyāna.....Twice.
Prāṇa, apāna, samāna, vyāna, udāna.....Once.
Apāna, vyāna, prāṇa, samāna, udāna.....Once.
Prāṇa, vyāna, apāna, samāna, udāna.....Four times.
Apāna, prāṇa..........................Four times.
Vyāna ....Once.

VII. Material in re the Prāṇa-Series in the Sūtra Literature.

Bloomfield's Concordance (in manuscript) and indexes to the Sūtras have made it possible to rapidly scrutinize a good deal of Sūtra literature. A single member of the Prāṇa-Series is frequently mentioned, the others being understood as following on—so entirely formulaic is the material. This is especially true of the Kāty. Çrāuta Sūtra. We have noted the following references in the Vāitāna, Kāuçika, Pāraskara Gṛhya, Mānava Gṛhya and Kātyāyana Çrāuta Sūtras.

Prāṇāpānāu ....Seven times.
Prāṇa, apāna, vyāna, samāna, udāna.....Once.
Prāṇa, vyāna, apāna, udāna, samāna.....Once.
Prāṇa, apāna ....Twice.
Prāṇa, vyāna ....Once.
Prāṇa, apāna, vyāna...................Once.
Prāṇāpānāu, samānavyānāu, udānarūpe..Twice.

Six instances where *prāṇa* introduces one or more of the remaining members of the Prāṇa-Series—the form having become thoroughly stereotyped.

CHAPTER II.

ATTEMPTS MADE BY HINDU SCHOLARS TO EXPLAIN THE PRĀṆA-SERIES.

In a systematic attempt to arrive at the method of interpreting the material just outlined, it seems fitting to first ascertain the views of Hindu writers as to the meaning and empiric application of the various terms used.

No serious attempt to explain the Prāṇa-Series, in whole or in part, is made in the literature where its use is most frequent, viz.: YV., AV., and ÇB. The manipulation of *pra* and *ā* in ÇB. i. 4. 1. 5, and similar passages is not to be taken too seriously. The Upaniṣads, however, offer several more or less thorough attempts at detailed explanation. No two explanations are in entire accord; in fact the differences are rather more marked than the agreements. This situation indicates an uncertainty as to the meaning originally intended no less marked than the uncertainty of modern scholars as shown by their divergencies of translation. The Hindu attempts at explanation may best be considered passage by passage in order that each may be carefully scrutinized and criticised.

Māitri Upaniṣad ii. 6.

Prajāpati, having transformed himself into wind (*vāyu*), determined to enter into the creatures which he had made for the purpose of animating them (*pratibodhanāya*), seeing that they were as yet lifeless. As single, he (Prajāpati-Vāyu) could not do this, so he divided himself into five parts, becoming *prāṇa*, *apāna*, *samāna*, *udāna*, and *vyāna*.

Prāṇa ascends upwards—*ūrdhvam utkrāmati.*

Apāna moves downward—*avāñ saṁkrāmati.*

Vyāna is that by which these (*prāṇa* and *apāna*) are supported (*anugṛhītā*).

Samāna is that which conducts into *apāna*—*apāne prāpayati*—the grossest element of food and distributes—*samānayati*—the subtile (elements of food) into the various portions of the body—*añge añge*. It (*samāna*) is a higher form of *vyāna*—*uttaraṁ vyānasya rūpam*,—and between them is the production (or rise) of *udāna*—*cāi 'teṣām antarā prasūtir evo 'dānasya.*

Udāna is that which ejects or belches forth—*udgirati*—and swallows down—*nigirati*—that which is drunk and eaten.

In the note of explanation which is interposed between the definitions of *samāna* and *udāna* and begins, "*uttaram vyānasya*," we would differ somewhat from Cowell. He translates, but without reason as it seems to us, thus: "The *vyāna* comes after the others and the rise of the *udāna* is interposed before it."

The meaning of the passage as we have translated it is not without obscurity, but it is certainly less obscure than the rendering Cowell gives, and it has, moreover, the advantage, as we believe, of representing the text as it stands.

In the case of each of the definitions, the name of the thing defined comes after the definition, and the name is introduced by "*eṣa vāva sa.*" In the case of *samāna*, the "*eṣa vāva sa*" sentence is lengthened out so as to define it (*samāna*) in its relation to the names which precede and follow: *eṣa vāva sa samānasaṁjñā uttaraṁ vyānasya rūpaṁ cāi 'teṣām antarā prasūtir evo 'dānasya,* "Verily this one named *samāna* is a higher form of *vyāna,*" etc. There is no break in thought between *samānasaṁjñā* and *uttaraṁ*, etc.

The above definitions enable us to characterize with some degree of accuracy the writer's position.

1. *Prāṇa* and *apāna* do not stand for the two simple breath movements up-breathing and down-breathing or *vice versa.* On the contrary, we have here the point of view for which certain passages of the ÇB. form the basis, viz.: that there are two main movements of the breath, one upwards from the navel, the other downwards.

Prāṇa, therefore, includes both inhalation and exhalation, while *apāna* refers to that movement of breath which takes place in the evacuation both of excrement, and urine and semen. Careful observation of one's own sensations, in connection with these bodily functions, especially when effort is required or experimentally used, will reveal the impression of a downward movement of the air which has been inhaled. This sensation is doubtless the empiric basis of the above definition. The use of the word *apāna* in the same section to describe the place where the grossest parts of food go, renders the explanation of *apāna,* which has just been given, entirely certain. In this use of the word Cowell translates it by "lower bowel." It is not possible to decide finally whether the reference is to the "lower bowel" or to the air or "breath" which moves in the lower bowel. The contrast between "*añge añge*" and *apāna* suggests, however, that Cowell is right and that the meaning has passed over from "the air which moves in the lower bowel" to the lower bowel itself.

2. *Udāna,* as described, seems to refer to eructation. This the people of India consider to be a phenomenon of good digestion at the present day. Belching is looked upon as "good form" and is reckoned to be a sure sign that the food or drink just consumed will digest properly. The first of the two verbs used in the definition frequently means "to vomit." The use of the verbs side by side, however, points to the phenomenon of eructation.

3. *Samāna*, according to this writer, is the breath which carries on the process of digestion. The verb may be a compound of $\sqrt{n\bar{\imath}}$ with *sam* and *ā* or it may be the denominative of the noun or adjective *samāna*, or again it can be, as Whitney makes it, the causative of $\sqrt{an}$ with *sam*. The most probable of the three possibilities seems to us to be the second. The noun *samāna* is taken as the basis, while, at the same time, in the intended meaning, there is a play upon the adjective *samāna*, meaning "same" or "like." Perhaps the most striking phenomenon of the animal organism is that of digestion. It was sure to be identified with one of the commonly assumed breath processes. *Samāna* is readily suggested by the adjective *samāna* whose meaning fits in with what takes place in digestion. The mere conception is a sufficient argument; lo, the thing is done! The identification is complete and *samāna* makes equal (*samānayati*), or assimilates food and drink. If the verb be $\sqrt{n\bar{\imath}}$, plus *sam* and *ā*, there is still to be understood a play upon both adjective and noun.

This is really a brilliant example of that fanciful etymologizing in which the Hindu excels, doubtless because of his theory of the power inherent in each syllable of articulate sounds.

4. *Vyāna* is that breath which is always present even when there is no breath activity either upward or downward (cf. Ch. Up. i. 3. 3), and therefore, both *prāṇa* and *apāna* may be said to depend upon it.

5. The sense in which *samāna* is a higher form of *vyāna* is confessedly obscure, but it may be suggested tentatively that while the latter represents the breath ever present in the body merely as the support of *prāṇa* and *apāna*, the former is the same breath considered as active in the digestive process.

6. The sense in which *udāna* is looked upon as between *vyāna* and *samāna* is also quite uncertain. May not the allusion be to the phenomenon of eructation, which we have seen to be identified with *udāna*, since it takes place after food and before digestion? As *samāna* is *vyāna* engaged in digestion and as *vyāna* is, of course (cf. definition), present before and while food is being taken, therefore, it is not impossible to conceive that it is in this sense that *udāna* is between *vyāna* and *samāna*.

There is, to be sure, nothing very profound in our author's meaning, if we have rightly interpreted him; but this need not surprise us—in fact, the demand for profundity must be avoided as a snare in the interpretation of literature of this type.

Amṛtabindu Upaniṣad, 32–35.

32. *triṇçatparvā 'ñgulaḥ prāṇo yatra prāṇaḥ pratiṣṭhitaḥ,*
eṣa prāṇa iti khyāto bāhyaprāṇaḥ sagocaraḥ.

"Thirty thumb-breadths is the *prāṇa* (from) where the *prāṇa* is located. The *prāṇa*, thus named, has the external *prāṇa* (the sun) as its correlate (*sagocaraḥ*—having-a-with-sphere)."

33. This stanza describes the number of times breath is inhaled and exhaled within the period of a day and a night. The number is put at 113,680, "*açītiḥ ṣaṭçataṁ cāi 'va sahasrāṇi trayodaça lakṣaç cai 'kaḥ.*" This number is probably to be divided by five (cf. Deussen *in loco*), since five breaths are mentioned below and each one is doubtless supposed to have the same number of movements. This is certainly true with reference to in-breathing and out-breathing and is analogically assumed in the case of the others. The above number divided by five gives 22,736 or 15.9 per minute. The Haṅsa Up. (iv.), as Deussen has pointed out, puts the number at 21,606; the Sarva Darçana (page 175), at 21,600, and Rāmatīrtha in his notes to Māitri Up. vi. 1, at 21,000. For a fanciful theory of the numbers of *prāṇas* and *anas*, cf. ÇB. xii. 3. 2. 5. All these numbers are approximately accurate. It is probable that one or more of these numbers were ascertained by actual count. A Hindu Saṁnyāsin would think his time well spent in counting the number of his respirations. On the other hand, some of these totals have the appearance of having been made up to suit some theory as to how many there ought to be.

It is important to compare here Māitri Up. vi. 1. There *prāṇa* and the sun[1] are called the inner and outer (*antar bahiç ca*) paths of the Supreme Ātman. They are both said to revolve in a day and a night and the one is measured by the other. Now from the fact that the measurements are given in stanza 33, it seems certain that in stanza 32 *bāhyaprāṇa* means the sun and that, therefore, Māitri Up. vi. 1 ff. and the present passage deal with the same subject.

The first half of stanza 32 is somewhat obscure. Probably the statement is intended to apply to distance from the navel to the mouth. Thirty thumbs-breadths is an approximately accurate measurement of this distance. The navel is looked upon as the

---

[1] The Stoics taught a divine Pneuma (*prāṇa*) in the sun. Windelband, *Hist. of Phil.*, p. 39.

centre from which the breath divides to go upward or downward, and it is definitely represented as the place of the breath, cf. Kṣurika Up. 7. Since the breath movements are to be numbered in the following stanza (33), it is not very surprising that the exuberant fancy of a Hindu writer should think of the distance which, according to his idea of the starting point, breath travels at each inhalation and exhalation. Deussen adopts the emendation of the Telugu edition and reads the line, "*triṅçadvarddhāñguliḥ prāṇo yatra prāṇāiḥ pratiṣṭhitaḥ,* etc." This does not seem to be necessary, nor is the meaning as satisfactory as may appear at first sight. On the other hand, the heart is said to be the knot (*granthi*) of the *prāṇas,*[1] cf. TĀ. x. 37, 1, Gobhila Gṛh. Sūtra ii. 10, 28. For the relation between the heart and the *prāṇas,* cf. also ÇB. iii. 8. 3. 15; Ch. Up. iii. 12; Muṇḍ. Up. ii. 1. 8; Çiras Up. iii. (=Brahma Up. ii.); Amṛtabindu Up. 34; Bṛh. Ār. iv. 4. 1; Māitri Up. ii. 6.

On the other hand, the heart-cavity (*guha*) is said again and again to be the dwelling place of the Ātman or Puruṣa, variously described, cf. Kaṭha Up. ii. 20; iii. 1; v. 3; vi. 17; Ch. Up. viii. 3. 3; Māitri Up. vi. 34; vii. 7; Bṛh. Ār. Up. v. 8. 1; ii. 1. 17; Tāitt. Up. i. 6. 1; Ch. Up. iii. 14. 3.

But if the heart is meant, where, according to Deussen, the *prāṇa* dwells with the *prāṇas,* the measurement given, viz: "Dreissig Mannsfinger breit Raum ist, etc.," is entirely too large. Though the text we have used and the translation we have given are full of difficulties, yet they yield results suited to the context. It may be noted that Deussen has not appreciated the reference to the sun in the second half of the stanza.

34–35. (a) The preceding stanzas are preliminary; it is here that we find a definite attempt to explain the Prāṇa-Series:

prāṇa ādyo hṛdi sthāne apānas tu punar gude,
samāno nābhideçe tu udānaḥ kaṇṭham āçritaḥ.
vyānaḥ sarveṣu cā'ñgeṣu sadā vyāvṛtya tiṣṭhati.

"*Prāṇa* has its location in the heart. *Apāna* is located in the lower bowel. *Samāna* is located in the navel-region. *Udāna* abides in (or has recourse to) the throat. *Vyāna,* divided up, (*vyāvṛtya*) abides always in all the members."

[1] Compare the doctrine of the Stoics that seven pneumata (*prāṇas*) extend out from the heart like the arms of a polyp. The seven are made up of the five senses, the faculty of speech and the organ of procreation. Ibid., p. 189.

The writer makes his position clear as far as it goes.

1. In locating *prāṇa* in the heart he follows the oft-repeated assertion that the heart is the home of the *prāṇa* and the *prāṇas.*

2. In his opinion as to *apāna* he agrees in part with Māitri Up. ii. 6. He describes *apāna* as in the lower bowel, but does not identify it therewith.

3. The "navel-region" is a term broad enough to include the place of digestion. In locating *samāna* therein, our author is not necessarily out of agreement with the writer of Māitri Up. ii. 6. The definition, however, looks especially towards ÇB. viii. 3. 1. 6 and 10, where *samāna* is identified with the navel region.

4. The location of *udāna* in the throat is a corroboration of the interpretation given in the Māitri passage. In eructation the sensation is of breath ascending to the throat and returning to the stomach. In this we have the empiric starting point of the view which, as further developed, locates *udāna* in the Suṣumṇā or great artery, and assumes that it is the breath which carries the soul to the crown of the head in the true Yogin state—in fact identifies it (*udāna*) with the artery by which the soul departs from the body at death, i. e. with the Suṣumṇā.

5. The explanation of *vyāna* keeps in mind the prefix *vi.* The same prefix is used in the accompanying gerund, *vyāvṛtya,* and the assertion that *vi-āna* is in all members is made in allusion to *vi* as meaning "apart," "asunder," etc.

This definition illumines the statement in Māitri ii. 6, that *samāna* is the *uttara* form of *vyāna.* Since *vyāna* is in all the members and *samāna* apportions food to all the members, the latter may be fittingly called the superior form of the former.

Stanzas 35b–37 describe the colors of these *prāṇas.* The whole is too fanciful to merit our attention at this time.

Praçna Upaniṣad iii.

This section contains the most complete attempt of Hindu literature to define the members of the Prāṇa-Series. The five *prāṇas* are explained both microcosmically and macrocosmically.

The section begins with five questions as to *Prāṇa,* which is here the aggregate of the life-functions, viewed as a separate entity, distinct from the body—in other words, the Soul.

1. Whence does this *Prāṇa* arise?
2. How does it come into the body?

3. Having divided itself, how is it located? Read *prātiṣṭhate* for *pratiṣṭhate*, cf. PW.

4. By what does it go out (*utkramate*)?

5. How is it to be explained (*abhidhatte*) with reference (a) to the external world (*bāhyam*), and (b) to the individual organism (*adhyātmam*)?

The replies given are as follows:

(1) It is produced (*jāyate*) from Ātman. "As the shadow in man, the one in the other is diffused"—*yathāi 'ṣā puruṣe chāyāi 'tasminn etad ātatam.*

(2) It comes into the body apart from the activity of the mind or will (*mano 'kṛtena*)—literally, "By means of a non-acting *manas.*" Çañkara in his interpretation neglects the *a* before *kṛtena* and so attributes the coming of the *Prāṇa* into the body as the result of works done through *manas*, cf. Deussen *in loco.*

(3) In the answer to the third question, the Prāṇa-Series is directly dealt with. The reply begins with the declaration that as a king stations his subordinates in one town and another, each separately, so *Prāṇa* assigns to the various members of the Series their separate places in the body, as follows:

(a) *Prāṇa* assigns *apāna* to the anus and sexual organ—*pāyūpasthe 'pānam prātiṣṭhate.*

(b) It assigns itself—*svayam*—to eye and ear along with (or, from) mouth and nostrils—*cakṣuḥçrotre mukhanāsikābhyām.*

(c) *Samāna*, however, is in the middle—*madhye tu samānaḥ.* This it is that leads to homogeneity—"*samannayati*"—the offered food—*hutam annam.* From that (i. e. food), these seven flames arise, cf. the seven "*jihvāḥ*" or "*homāḥ*" of Mahānār. Up. x. 2; and Muṇḍ. Up. ii. 1. 8. Are the five senses, speech and procreation referred to?

(d) *Vyāna* functions—*carati*—in the 101 veins (*nāḍī*) whose location is in the heart where the Ātman is. These veins are each divided into 100 parts and these again into 72,000 parts each (ib. 6).

In this passage, we have both a combination of Ch. Up. viii. 6. 6 (101 veins[1]) and Bṛh. Ār. Up. ii. 1. 19 (72,000 veins called

---

[1] For other literature in re the Hitās or Nāḍīs, cf. Kāuṣ. Up., iv. 19; Āit. Up. ii. 1. 6; Ch. Up. viii. 6. 1-6; Bṛh. Ār. Up., iv. 2. 3; iv. 3. 20; Muṇḍ. Up. ii. 2. 6; Brahmavidyā Up. xii.; Kṣur. Up. 8, 9, 17, etc.; Mahānār. Up. xi. 8; Kaṭha Up. vi. 16; ÇB. i. 4. 1. 24; iv. 1. 2. 3; iv. 3. 1. 23; iv. 4. 1. 1; vii. 5. 1. 21.

"*hitāḥ*") and a still further fanciful division into the extreme of number and minuteness. The whole number becomes 727, 210, 201.

In Brahmavidyā Up. xii., 72,000 veins are apparently merged into the Suṣumṇā. Such a conception is the counterpart and possibly the original of the scheme which divides each by 72,000.

(e) *Udāna* is the one which (goes) upward, and by means of good leads to a good world, by evil to an evil world; by (a combination of) the two to the world of man. With reference to these replies, the following points are to be observed:

1. *Apāna* is described essentially as in Māitri Up. ii. 6.

2. *Prāṇa* is used in two senses, neither of which corresponds to its use in the passages already considered. The *Prāṇa*, which is the main subject of the chapter, is a synonym of Brahman, and recalls the Prajāpati-Vāyu of Māitri Up. ii. 6, which divided itself up into the five members of the Prāṇa-Series.

Again, the *prāṇa* as assigned to its place in the body is a conception very different from the simple breath-activity found in previous explanations. In fact our author in having *prāṇa* assigned by *Prāṇa*, passes over from the Prāṇa-Series as such to a conception which belongs elsewhere. The assignment of *prāṇa* is clearly to the seven "openings in the head" which we shall find again and again referred to as "the seven *prāṇas*." Since the *prāṇas* are all manifestations of the central *Prāṇa*, they are described as a unit. This gives an appearance of consistency to the writer's treatment of the series of five. It is not possible to say positively whether the dual for mouth-nostrils is an instrumental or an ablative. If the latter, we may recognize here an interesting anatomical reference to the Eustachian tubes and lachrymal ducts. More probably, however, we have here the instrumental of accompaniment and, as already intimated, a definite allusion to the "seven *prāṇas* in the head."

3. *Samāna* is very much as in Māitri Up. ii. 6. The point of the argument is a play on the words *samāna* and *sama*, the latter being the form used with the root $\sqrt{n\bar{\imath}}$ to form the *samannayati*.

4. In the explanation of *vyāna*, the statement of Amṛtabindu Up. that *vyāna* abides always in all the members of the body, receives a further and entirely fanciful development. The innumerable divisions of the veins, in which *vyāna* functions, is another way of saying that *vyāna* is in every fibre of the body.

5. The presentation of *udāna* is unique and difficult. A clue to the understanding of the author's meaning is, we think, to be found by recalling what is taught regarding the great vein Suṣumṇā, which is said to extend from the heart to the crown of the head. In the complete concentration inculcated by the Yoga philosophy, the soul is theoretically made to ascend by this passage-way until it reaches the crown of the head or a point between the eyebrows; cf. Dhyānabindu Up. 13–23, and Nādabindu Up. iv. By this same great vein the soul ascends and passes out at death; cf. Kṣur. Up.; Māitri Up. vi. 21; Āit. Up. i. 3, 12; Kaṭha Up. vi. 5. We have seen above (Amṛtab. and Māitri Ups.) that *udāna* is the breath of eructation and is located in the throat. This gives us the conception of a breath that ascends (*ud*) and prepares the way for what we have here. If any one of the five breaths is to be conceived of as functioning in the Suṣumṇā, the prefix *ud* of *udāna* would be sufficient to determine that the choice should fall upon it. We already have *udāna* extending as far as the neck, and further Hindu fancy did not find it difficult to take another step and completely identify *udāna* and Suṣumṇā. It may be that we have the basis of the conception in AV. xi. 9, 21, where the *prāṇa* is said to escape upwards in the article of death. This need not, however, be pressed.

6. The description of *udāna*, given above, is in answer to the fourth question, "By what does it (the *Prāṇa*) go out?"

The fifth question is answered in part by the reply given to the third query, since said reply tells how *Prāṇa* functions in the individual organism; cf. Question 5.

Later, however, the fifth question is systematically answered by a statement of cosmic correlates of each of the five breaths.

(a) The sun rises as the external *Prāṇa* (*bāhyaḥ prāṇaḥ*, cf. Amṛtab. Up. 32), supporting that *prāṇa* in the eye.[1]

(b) The divinity which is in the earth is the one which supports, *avaṣṭabhya*, the *apāna* of man.

(c) *Samāna* is the space, *ākāça*, between (sun and earth).

(d) *Vyāna* is Vāyu.

(e) *Udāna* is the fire-element (*tejas*). "By it (*udāna*) a man becomes one whose fire-element is extinguished, i. e. dies—*tasmād*

---

[1] So conceived because in seeing, as in other psychical acts, the Supreme Prāṇa is the active agent and so can be said to dwell in the eye. This conception is accentuated by the wonderful character of the eye. The "Man in the eye" figures largely in Hindu thought.

upaçāntatejāḥ. Whatever thought (determination) is re-born along with (or by) the fusing of the senses into the organ of intellect (*manas*)—by it he goes to *prāṇa*. *Prāṇa*, united with the fire-element, (and) accompanied by Ātman leads to the predetermined world."

These statements of correlation are full of interest.

1. The connection between the sun and the eye-*prāṇa* is a correlation which from its frequency may be called formative and structural. The number of allusions which rest upon the conception that the eye is to the body what the sun is to the universe, is very large. The myth of the Heavenly Eye-ball crystallizes this conception in an interesting way. First the sun and the eye are correlated. Again, since the sun is but one form of the heavenly light of which lightning is another, the eye and lightning are correlated, VS. xxv. 1, 2. The third step is to posit an eye and an eye-ball to the sun or to the lightning. A still further step leads to the myth proper, according to which the eye and the eye-ball of the sun and lightning, or of anthropomorphic divinities substituted for them, are described as descending to the earth and becoming various useful and pleasing objects. Plants especially are identified with this heavenly eye-ball; cf. Bloomfield's "Interpretation of the Veda," Seventh Series, AJP. xvii., No. 4, p. 399 ff.

In this connection one can scarcely avoid recalling the genetic series of ÇB., ix. 3. 3. 15—lightning, rain plants—and the many similar statements to the same effect in other passages.

2. Since *apāna* has been located by *Prāṇa* in the anus and scrotum, "Divinity in the earth" is probably not Agni as might readily be assumed, but the expression is rather intended to describe the earth herself as personified; cf. RV. v. 84, and AV. xii. 1.

The main question is how the Earth-Divinity sustains (or, seizes—$\sqrt{stabh}$ with *ava* may mean either) the *apāna* of man. Do we not have here a reference to the simple every-day phenomenon according to which the earth both receives and absorbs both excrement and urine? Since by means of *apāna*, located in anus and scrotum, they are voided upon the earth, therefore the two are correlated; cf. ÇB. vi. 7. 1. 11; ĀB. ii. 6 (end); ÇB. x. 1. 1. 11.

3. The identification of *samāna* and *ākāça* (here as *antarikṣam*) is, from the cosmic standpoint, quite in harmony with the

location of the microcosmic *samāna* in the middle part or navel region of the body.

4. *Vyāna* as *Vāyu* also fits in well with the above noted definitions which emphasize the pervasiveness of *vyāna*.

The correlation has also the further advantage, dear to the Hindu author's ear, of being based upon a pun, *vāy* and *vyā*.

5. The correlation of *udāna* and *tejas* is unique and the explanation which follows it is obscure, at least when considered alone. Brief as it is, the explanation bristles with important allusions to structural conceptions.

The starting-point for an adequate interpretation of the passage is the fact that *udāna* (in the individual organism—*adhyātmam*) moves in the vein (*nāḍī*) which goes upward, i. e. the Suṣumṇā? Now psychical activity (*prāṇa*, cf. below) is a fire-element (*tejomātrā*). In Bṛh. Ār. Up. iv. 4. 1, the Çārīra Ātman is said to seize the *prāṇas* or fire-elements (*tejomātrāḥ*) and move down along to the heart—*hṛdayam evā 'nvavakrāmati*.

Further in Kāuṣ. Up. ii. 12, each psychical activity is said to be a form in which the Brahman flames up in the individual. Each activity is, therefore, a composite of *prāṇa* and *tejas*. When the said flame dies down, the *prāṇa*-element thereof goes into *Prāṇa* and the *tejas*-element passes into the psychical organ next in order of extinguishment. The whole statement may be summarized, as follows:

The *tejas* of speech goes to the eye; its *prāṇa* to Prāṇa.
The *tejas* of the eye goes to the ear; its *prāṇa* to Prāṇa.
The *tejas* of the ear goes to the *manas;* its *prāṇa* to Prāṇa.
The *tejas* of the *manas* goes to the Prāṇa; its *prāṇa* to Prāṇa.

Note that the net result is Prāṇa. This is a description of what takes place at death. Similar descriptions with other arrangements of the organs are frequently met with; cf. Speech, *manàs*, *prāṇa* and *tejas:* Ch. Up. vi. 8. 6; iv. 3. 3; Bṛh. Up. iii. 2. 13.

It is entirely clear that our author in his treatment of *udāna* is dealing with what takes place at death. At that time the fire-elements are all extinguished and only Prāṇa abides, i. e. the Supreme Prāṇa which is the main subject of the chapter. It is not to be forgotten, however, that we are dealing with the cosmical Tejas in the answer to question 5.

There are two alternatives here. Either the author has forgotten his assumed point of view and is now discussing a correlation restricted to the individual organism; or he means to imply that the Tejas of each organ is a cosmic product. The latter alternative is manifestly the more probable. Doubtless the Tejas with which *udāna* is correlated is the Agni-Brahman which flames up in each organ of psychical activity, cf. again Kāuṣ. Up. ii. 12. *Udāna* is, then, the cosmical Tejas in the sense that it absorbs the fire-elements as they appear in the separate psychical organ. There is here a two-fold identification of *udāna.* On the one hand, it is equivalent to the microcosmical *prāṇa* of Kāuṣ. Up. ii. 12, since into it are fused the fire-elements of the other organs. On the other hand, having absorbed the various fire-elements, it is said to be equivalent to that which it has absorbed, viz:—Tejas. A third identification of *udāna* has already been noted above, i. e. with the Suṣumṇā.

Beginning with *udāna* (above, *e*), a review of the death-process is given. The senses fuse into *manas.* This fusion leads to the formation (manner not explained) of a determining thought (*citta*),[1] which passes on into *prāṇa. Prāṇa* is now everything. The fire-elements of all the psychical organs are contained in it, and so it departs (by the *udāna*-Suṣumṇā), having the Ātman along (cf. Bṛh. Ār. Up. iv. 4. 3), one being as the shadow of the other (cf. answer to question 1)—thus going to the condition pre-determined by the "composite" thought, which forms itself in the mind when the senses are fused therein.

Praçna Up. iv. 3 and 4.

The Prāṇa-Series is here presented under a correlation which may fittingly be called *adhiyajñam*, i. e. "with reference to the sacrifice." Five questions begin the chapter.

(a) What (*kāni*) sleep in man?
(b) What (*kāni*) remain awake?
(c) Whose is that pleasure (*sukham*)?
(d) What god sees them sleeping?
(e) In whom are they all grounded (*sampratiṣṭhitāḥ*)?

The answers in brief are as follows:

(a) The ten organs of action—doubtless *karmāṇi* with *kāni.*
(b) The *prāṇa*-fires—*prāṇāgnayaḥ.*
(c) Manas.

---

[1] ÇB. vii. 1. 1. 24, the *prāṇas* are said to be the inspirers of all thoughts.

(d) The *manas* of the Vijñānātman Puruṣa.

(e) The highest Ātman.

In connection with the second answer three members of the Prāṇa-Series are correlated with the sacrificial fires (cf. ÇB. vii. 1. 2. 21), and the other two are forcibly brought into line with the sacrifice. *Apāna* is the Gārhapatya Fire, i. e. western. *Vyāna* is the Anvāhāryapacana Fire, i. e. southern. Prāṇa is the Āhavanīya Fire, i. e. eastern. To this simple correlation, definitions of *samāna* and *udāna* are added:

1. *Samāna* leads to homogeneity—*samaṁ nayati*—the two oblations, exhalation and inhalation, i. e. *ucchvāsaniçvāsāu.* The verb form is again new. We have already had *samānayati* and *samannayati.*

2. *Udāna* is the fruit of the sacrifice—*iṣṭaphalam.* It conveys the sacrificer (= Manas) to Brahman day by day.

Points of importance for our investigation are :

(a) The pun on *samāna* by using *samam* with *nayati.* Here it is the breath movements, not food, which are assimilated. It is a dominant Upaniṣad doctrine that the true sage performs the Agnihotra sacrifice when he accompanies the eating of food with the recital of Mantras to the various *prāṇas* cf. Prāṇāg. Up.; Ch. Up. v. 19–24, etc. Here it suits the purpose of the writer to leave the matter of food out of sight. He merely hints at, rather than states, the important doctrine just referred to. He is occupied with correlating the main facts of the actual sacrifice with the Prāṇa-Series. As the Prāṇa-Series belongs to the animal organism, he seeks for psychical functions which will correspond to the two oblations and finds them in the two main breath movements.

(b) A further hint towards the identification of *udāna* and Suṣumṇā. Day by day Manas, which is here the Vijñānātman Puruṣa, passes out by *udāna* and returns again. It is the "fruit of the sacrifice" by means of which the sacrificer reaches Brahman. This is the assumption which has to be manipulated into line with the Prāṇa-Series. In Bṛh. Ār. Up. iv. 3. 13, the Puruṣa= Ātman (= Manas here), is said to leave the body and roam about, *prāṇa* being left in charge during its absence. Some such conception controls the application of the Prāṇa-Series to the sacrifice. The great vein by which the Manas ascends performs the same office for the soul of the sage as the *iṣṭaphalam* does for the performer of the ritual sacrifice, hence *udāna* is the *iṣṭaphalam.*

(c) The correlation of *apāna, vyāna* and *prāṇa* with the West, South and East respectively, is in line with their usual arrangement in other parts of the literature; cf. below.

The Prāṇa-Series and the Points of the Compass.

The following passages, though furnishing no attempt at an explanation of the proper significance of the various terms, are yet of value as illustrating an interesting symbolic use of the members of the Series.

Ch. Up. iii. 13.

prāṇa. *vyāna.* *apāna.* *samāna.*
East (*prāñ*), South (*dakṣiṇaḥ*), West (*pratyañ*), North (*udañ*),
udāna.
Upper (*ūrdhvaḥ*).

This section contains also a series of both psychical and cosmical entities, which are correlated with the five names. They belong to a later phase of our subject; the correlations given above are manifestly symbolical. The pun between *prāṇa* and *prāñ* furnishes the starting point, and the others are made to fall in line. It is rather surprising to find that *udāna* and *udañ* are *not* correlated.

Pāraskara Gṛhya Sūtra i. 16. 9-15.

Shortly after a son has been born, five Brahmans sit down around him. Then to each one in turn the father says, *imam anuprāṇita.* In obedience to this injunction they speak in turn, as follows:

The one on the east says "Prāṇa." The one on the south says "Vyāna." The one on the west says "Apāna." The one on the north says "Udāna." The fifth, looking up, says "Samāna."

Here, as we should expect, *udāna* and *udañ* are correlated.

ÇB. xi. 8. 3. 6.

Here the various directions (*diças*) are represented as putting their corresponding vital breath into the dead sacrificial victim:

The eastern quarter puts in the *prāṇa.*
The southern quarter puts in the *vyāna.*
The western quarter puts in the *apāna.*
The northern quarter puts in the *udāna.*
The upper (zenith) quarter puts in the *samāna.*

Each quarter is represented as giving first a command in which the imperative mood of each member of the Prāṇa-Series is in turn used, e. g. *tam prācī dik prāṇe 'ty anuprāṇat prāṇam evā 'smiṅs tad adadhāt.* Note that in this same passage, the ceremony described in Pār. Gṛh. Sūtra i. 16. 9-15, is said to take place before the umbilicus is cut.

Upaniṣad Definition of Single Members of the Prāṇa-Series.

The above attempts at explanation have dealt with the entire series of names. There are, however, a few references in which single members of the Prāṇa-Series are more or less specifically defined.

APĀNA.

1. In Māitri Up. ii. 6, *apāna* is defined so as to mean the intestine.
2. In Garbha Up. i., it is said to be used in evacuation (*utsarge*).
3. The following stanza occurs in Saṁnyāsa Up. 2(5).:

vṛṣaṇāpānayor madhye pāṇī āsthāya saṁçrayet,
saṁdaçya daçanāir (or, *çanakair*) *jihvāṁ yavamātre vinirgatām.*

The context deals with the phenomenon of death. At such a time and, indeed at any time it is natural that the hands when folded should rest between the scrotum and the navel. *Apāna*, therefore, probably means "the navel" here, and not the anus as in the former references. The writer is possibly referring back to a passage now to be noted.

3. Āit. Up. i. 1 and 2. *Apāna* is used here twice. The subject is creation by the Supreme Ātman. The two sections describe respectively, (a) The formation of the psychical organs (called "world-protectors"—*lokapālāḥ*) by the application of heat to a primeval man, taken out of the waters. (b) The entrance of each separate organ into man.

The assertion of the first section in which we are interested is that after the navel had burst forth (*nirabhidyata*), *apāna* burst forth from the navel and from *apāna*, death.

In the description of the reverse of the process, death becoming *apāna*, is said to enter the navel. Now it is by no means easy to understand what point of view is assumed in making death the cosmical counterpart of *apāna*. The other correlations of the passage, viz: Speech and fire; breath and wind; eyes and sun; ears and quarters; hairs and shrubbery, etc.; *manas* (from heart and) moon: organ of generation from (semen and) waters: —are more or less familiar, but this is unique.

One can but suspect that the empiric basis of this correlation is found in certain of the phenomena of death. It is well known, at least to the medical profession, that the approach of death is heralded by rapid abdominal breathing after the chest muscles have ceased to act. The Hindus, inveterate observers as they were, could not have failed to note this phenomenon, and it is quite in keeping with their method that some one should have inferred therefrom that some connection exists between death and the navel region.

Again, in the final moment, the last gasp is a breathing-out, in other words an *apāna* movement, for such is the dominant meaning of the word (cf. below). After the last gasp the abdomen, which a little before was moving rapidly, becomes still. Death has come, and the evidence of his arrival was a final *apāna*, i. e. the expulsion of breath from the navel-region. It seems probable that it was by some such steps that death, *apāna*, and the navel were connected.

4. Āit. Up. i. 3. When the Ātman created food, each psychical organ in turn, viz: Speech, *prāṇa*, eye, ear, skin, *manas*, organ of generation and *apāna*, strove to seize it. *Apāna* alone succeeded, hence it is called the "seizer of food" (*annasya grahaḥ*). The mention of *apāna* after the organ of generation suggests that *apāna* refers to the breath in the lower intestine and not to the navel. But even so, this does not seem to adequately cover the conception found in the phrase "seizer of food." It may be that *apāna* here refers not only to the breath as carrying away the rejected parts of food, but includes the activity of breath in the digestion of food as well. This suggestion makes *apāna* include both *samāna* and *apāna* of Māitri Up. ii. 6. Deussen's suggestion that *apāna* means "Princip der Verdauung" interprets the conception in part, but it does not take note of the probability that *apāna* as scrotum or as breath in the lower bowel gives the clue to an understanding of the author's point of view (cf. below).

It may be noted that in Pāras. Gṛh. Sūtra i. 19. 4, *prāṇa* is said to attain food, and *apāna* to attain scent. The question of *apāna* and scent, the importance of which is seen in its bearing upon the proper translation of *prāṇa* and *apāna*, will be discussed later.

VYĀNA.

Ch. Up. i. 3. 3 and 5.

In these references, *vyāna* is described as the connecting link or factor (*saṁdhi*) between *prāṇa* and *apāna*. As such, it is identified with speech, for "while one is speaking there is neither in-breathing nor out-breathing." This description tallies with the literal meaning of the word *vyāna*, i. e. "breathing apart." There is, so this author thinks, no movement of breath while words are being uttered, but merely a use of an abiding breath which supplies the basis for *prāṇa* and *apāna;* cf. Kāuṣ. Up. ii. 5.

Section 5 refers to other actions which are performed without *prāṇa* or *apāna* and, therefore, with *vyāna*. The actions named are: The production of fire by the churning-sticks, i. e. friction; running a race; and the stringing of a strong bow. It is difficult to understand how a race could be run without *prāṇa* and *apāna*. The allusion is doubtless to the final sudden spurt of a race. The above is a most interesting instance of acute observation. An occidental observer never stops to notice that in lifting a weight all breath action is held in abeyance. The Hindu, noticing it, has even given it a name. *Vyāna* is, therefore, the breath that permanently pervades the body (cf. Amṛtab. Up. 35), and continues when there is no breath-movement to or from the lungs.

Résumé of Hindu Attempts to Explain the Prāṇa-Series.

1. *Prāṇa* is the breath which moves upward from the navel or heart and includes both in-breathing and out-breathing. It is found in all the seven apertures of the head.

2. *Apāna* is a term of varying signification. It means

(1) The breath in the anus and scrotum. (2) The lower intestine. (3) The navel. (4) The "seizer of food," including both digestion and the carrying away of excrement.

3. *Vyāna* is the breath which pervades the members of the body, and in which *prāṇa* and *apāna* inhere.

4. *Udāna* is in part etymologically interpreted and refers

(1) To eructation. (2) To the breath which carries the soul up to the skull in the state of Samādhi, and on out in death. It is not only supposed to move in a great vein which extends from the centre of the body to the top of the head, but is identified with this vein.

5. *Samāna* is located in the abdomen and is said to bring about the digestion of food.

CHAPTER III.

Interpretation of the Prāṇa-Series.

An adequate interpretation of the Prāṇa-Series as a whole, or the individual members thereof, involves a review of the whole mass of material (Chap. i., B.), and a careful scrutiny of all the important references. Such an investigation will not only bring out the origin and value of the explanations given by Hindu writers (cf. Chap. ii.), but should also throw light upon the empiric origin and formulaic development of the series of names—thus leading to an insight into the question of translation as will serve to bring some degree of order into the confusion which now exists (cf. Chap. i., A.).

The purpose, thus outlined, may best he accomplished by a separate treatment of the various strata of literary deposit.

I. The Prāṇa-Series in the Vedas.

A. The Rig-Veda; cf. Introductory Chapter.

In the Rig-Veda, *prāṇa* means simply "breath," the prefix having no directional value. In the single passage where the participle of $\sqrt{}$*an* with *apa* is accompanied by the ablative of *prāṇa* (RV. x. 189. 2), nothing very definite as to the force of *apa* can be determined. It would seem, however, that the participle makes the compound mean "breathing off or forth." In any case the directional force, whatever it is, is not in *pra*, but in *apa*.

B. The Atharva-Veda.

The AV. frequently uses *prāṇa* and *apāna* together, usually as a copulative compound. *Prāṇa* alone means the vital act of breathing and it may, therefore, be assumed that in the compound *prāṇāpānāu*, *prāṇa* refers to that which is distinctively the vital act. That this is inhalation is at once axiomatic and scientific; and, therefore, the strongest probability of correctness attaches to the usual translation of the compound as "in-breathing and out-breathing." If the process of breathing be divided, the two movements just described will be the result. They fittingly form a dual compound, for they are a pair of constant value.

Wherever, from Veda to Sūtra, this compound occurs, it has the meaning given above. Any modifications which have occurred were only possible after the compound was divided. Not that "*prāṇa* and *apāna*," in the beginning or as a usual thing, meant anything different from *prāṇāpānāu*. The two forms stand side by side and are of equal value; cf. AV. vii. 53. 2–6, etc. At the same time, when the two words were released from the close relationship of dual compound, the way was open for modifications of meaning to take place. There was nothing to hinder *prāṇa* from again becoming an inclusive term for both the simple breath movements, while *apāna* was thus free to take on special meanings. AV. xiii. 3. 4, may indicate something of this kind:

yaḥ prāṇena dyāvāpṛthivī tarpayaty apānena samudrasya jaṭharaṁ yaḥ piparti, "Who with his *prāṇa* satisfies heaven and earth, and who with his *apāna* fills the belly of the ocean."

The hymn is to Rohita and describes the sun. One cannot be sure as to the direction in which the poet's fancy leads, and yet it seems probable that the line contains a hint at some definite conception of *apāna* as the downward moving breath. The idea of *apāna* as the breath which goes downward from the navel-region would not be incongruous here.

Twice in AV. xi. 4, the verbs $\sqrt{an}$ with *pra*, and $\sqrt{an}$ with *apa* are used side by side; cf. stanzas 8 and 14. In both cases the words seem to correspond precisely to the nouns as regards distinction of meaning. In describing the breathing of the embryo in the mother's womb, the usual order of the words is reversed and we have, *apāniti*, *prāṇiti*. This order may be intended to give expression to the fancy that the natural cycle of breath processes in the embryo is the reverse of what it is in all creatures which have come to birth.

In the translation of *vyāna* the AV. gives no assistance. In v. 4. 7, it occurs with *prāṇa* and the eye, just as in other stanzas *prāṇa-apāna*, eye, etc., are named. The line reads: "Be gracious unto my *prāṇa* and to my *vyāna* and to this eye of mine."

Again in AV. v. 2. 2, the participle of $\sqrt{an}$ with *vi* occurs both in its positive and negative forms, viz:—*avyanac ca vyanac ca*. The reference is to all creatures and the meaning is about equal to "inanimate and animate." The question which arises in these passages is whether *vyāna* has special significance, or is merely equal to *apāna* in the first reference, and whether in the second the participles are equivalent only to *aprāṇat* and *prāṇat*. The latter seems the more probable opinion. At the same time, it is likely that these passages furnish the basis for the definition of *vyāna* in Ch. Up. i. 3. 3 and 5, where *vyāna* is the breath which pervades the body apart from the two main breath movements. Such a meaning could be applied in both these passages. *Vyāna* occurs also in an obscure passage, i. e. AV. xiv. 1. 12 (cf. RV. x. 85. 12). The interpretation of the stanza is yet to be satisfactorily made. It will only be necessary here to quote the stanza and to note that, whatever be its interpretation, *vyāna* as therein used sheds its light on the meaning of the word in the Prāṇa-Series:

çucī te cakre yātyā vyāno akṣa āhataḥ
ano manasmayaṁ sūryā 'rohat prayatī patim.

If Sāyaṇa is right in assuming that the axle of the chariot is wind (Vāyu), then *vyāna* means "wind," and the reason for the poet's choice is to be found in the fact that *vyāna* is a pun both upon *vāyu* and *anas*.

Samāna occurs but once and sounds no note of distinct definition; it is purely formulaic.

Udāna occurs twice and in both cases is a member of the compound *vyānopānāu*, made after the analogy of *prāṇāpānāu*. This indicates that the breath names have already become crystallized into formulas. and formulas yield no valuable secrets of the kind we are searching for.

The verb $\sqrt{an}$ with *ud* is found in AV. iii. 13. 5, in the form *udāniṣuḥ*. The mighty ones are said to have "breathed up." The mighty ones are the waters and the breathing up occurs when Indra sets his feet upon them. Can there be here a reference to the tides?

C. The Yajur-Veda.

All the references are manifestly formulaic and contribute nothing to our purpose. The birds-eye view of the material given in the first chapter, B, above, tells the whole story.

II. The Prāṇa-Series in the Çatapatha Brāhmaṇa.

A striking feature of the ÇB. material, a summary of which has already been given, is the entire disappearance of *prāṇāpānāu*. The use of *prāṇa* and *apāna* is, moreover, very infrequent. We have noted but seven occurrences; only three of the seven being in the first ten books.

The place of the dual compound *prāṇāpānāu* is taken by *prāṇodānāu*, which occurs forty-one times. Again, when three members of the Series are mentioned, two of which are *prāṇa* and *vyāna*, the third is not *apāna*, as our experience of all the other literature would lead us to expect, but *udāna* instead. Not that the ordinary triplet does not occur. We have, in fact, noted six instances thereof; but they are all quotations from the Vāj. Saṁh.

These facts invite the conclusion that, from the view-point of ÇB., *apāna* as "out-breathing" has surrendered its place to *udāna*. With reference to this change, it may be suggested that of the two words, *apāna* and *udāna*, the latter, etymologically considered, was looked upon as better fitted to describe—the process of "out-breathing." Both words were already in existence; the interests of definiteness suggested that a choice should be made, and therefore the latter was chosen. By means of this surrender of place, the way was opened for *apāna* to be given a new meaning such as we have already pointed out as found in the Upaniṣads, viz:—the breath which moves downward from the middle of the body into the anus and sexual organ. Indeed the change we are considering may have been motived by this conception. It may be more accurate to say that *apāna* was coming to be wanted for a new purpose and, therefore, the field was given to *udāna*. The building of the Fire-altar, which was conceived of as a living creature, led to a mode of representation which at least looked towards a new use of *apāna*. As *prāṇa* connotes "life," there must be *prāṇas* in every part of the creature-like Fire-altar which was built up by the priests in connection with an elaborate ritual. Hence in ÇB. viii. 1. 3. 6, there is said to be one *prāṇa* in front (*purastāt*), another behind (*paçcāt*), another to the right (*dakṣiṇatas*), another to the left (*uttaratas*), and another in the middle (*madhye*). The names of these in their order are: *prāṇa*, *apāna*, *vyāna*, *udāna*, and *samāna*.

Sections 8 and 9 go on to describe the laying of the bricks. *Prāṇa* in front is connected with *apāna* by laying the rear or western bricks immediately after the front or eastern ones. In the same way *vyāna* and *udāna* are connected by laying the bricks of the left or north immediately after those of the right or south. Further, in section 10 the *prāṇa* which is put in the middle is called the intestinal breath (*gudaḥ*[1] *prāṇaḥ*). It is said to be placed round the navel lengthwise and crosswise, since the body breaths are in touch with each other lengthwise and crosswise.

This description in which *apāna* is clearly identified with *paçcāt prāṇa*, when combined with ÇB. iii. 8. 2. 6, where the anus is plainly called *paçcāt prāṇa*, accounts for the identification of *apāna* and the anus in Māitri Up. ii. 6; Amṛtab. Up. 34; and Praçna Up. iii. When the sacrifice is personified as a human being, the name *avāñ prāṇa* takes the place of *paçcāt prāṇa*. The change is due to the observation that the passage from mouth to anus follows a downward course, while in birds and beasts it is on the whole horizontal. Just as breath moves up and out by the mouth, so also does it move downward and out by the anus and scrotum. In ÇB. vii. 1. 2. 15, we find the following statement:

Prajātir eva yad ete 'vāñcaḥ prāṇā yad dhi mūtraṁ karoti yat purīṣam prai 'va taj jāyate.

"A procreation indeed are these downward breaths. Whatever urine or faeces he makes, it is they that produce them."

In ÇB. xii. 1. 4. 3; xii. 2. 4. 16; and xii. 3. 1. 8, these two downward breaths are called *go* and *āyus*. Doubtless *āyus*, i. e. "life," refers to the organ of procreation; and *go*, which may mean "earth," to the organ of evacuation. Again, in ÇB. i. 4. 3. 8, two breaths are said to go upward and two downward from the central breath. We shall have occasion to note later that of the nine *prāṇas* in the body two are said to be below (i. e. *avāñcāu*). Further in ÇB. vi. 7. 1. 11, that which is above the navel is immortal and streams out by upward breaths (*ūrdhvāiḥ prāṇair*), while what is mortal passes below the navel (*parāk tan nābhim atyeti*). The adverb properly means "turned away." Doubtless the idea is "in the opposite direction," hence below. We should have expected *avāñ prāṇa* here, had there been any attempt at definite description.

---

[1] Cf. Amṛtabindu Up. 34, above, where *apāna* is in the *guda*. Here the word is used in the general sense of all intestines; there of the lower bowel or anus especially. There is no confusion between *samāna* and *apāna*, any more than between the intestines in general where digestion takes place, and the intestine which carries away what is digested; cf. Āit. Up. i. 3.

ÇB. vi. 1. 2. 11, and x. 1. 3. 1, refer to mortals being created from the downward breaths of Prajāpati; in ÇB. xi. 1. 6. 8, however, it is the Asuras who are said to be thus created. That *avāñ prāṇa*, when standing in the singular, refers to the anus, is further proven by ÇB. xi. 5. 2. 4, where the scrotum is named side by side with it. The passage gives a description of the parts of the body. Beginning from the mouth and going downward, *avāñ prāṇa* comes immediately after the scrotum. Again in ÇB. xi. 1. 6. 30, it is said that everything which enters the various other breaths meets in *avāñ prāṇa*. This is manifestly a reference to the fact that the lower intestine carries away excrement.

Now the fact that *udāna* has largely taken the place of *apāna* as the companion of *prāṇa*, greatly simplifies the question of the true translation of *prāṇa* in ÇB. It cannot mean "out-breathing" along with *udāna*, and Eggeling's translation must, therefore, be rejected. While the point is absolutely final only for the ÇB., it is one that should be reckoned with by those translators of Upaniṣads who would have "out-breathing" to be one of the meanings of *prāṇa*.

It is important to note that in the identification of three of the breaths with draughts (*grahas*) of Soma (i. e. *upāñçu*, *upāñçusavana*, and *antaryāma*), the Āit. Brāh. (ii. 21) has *prāṇa* and *apāna* where the ÇB. has *prāṇa* and *udāna*. Haug claims oral information as the basis for his assertion that in the ceremony along with the use of the words *prāṇaṁ yaccha*, breath is inhaled, while after repeating *apāṇaṁ yaccha* it is expelled forcibly through the nose; cf. Haug's Āit. Brāh., page 118, note.

The opposite view, held by Eggeling, is impossible, since his text contains *udāna*, which certainly cannot mean "in-breathing." Even if *apāna* could be shown, contrary to its etymology, to sometimes mean "in-breathing," there is no hope of such a showing for *udāna*. Eggeling has been led astray by the use of certain words of direction or of certain particles of formulaic value, which supplied to the ever-watchful eye and ear of the Hindu an opportunity to indulge in a pun upon the prefix *pra* of *prāṇa*. Such particles and words are:

(a) *Pra* as the first word of a quotation; cf. ÇB. i. 4. 1. 5. The particle in contrast with *pra* is *ā*. The text has *prāṇa* and *udāna*. *Ā* does not even fit *udāna*, and it would certainly be precarious, therefore, to force any lexical meaning of *pra* into the word *prāṇa;* cf. Haug's Āit. Brāh. iii. 26.

In Āit. Ār. ii. 1. 5. 1, there is a combined play upon *prātāyi* (√*tan* with *pra*), *prātar* and *prāṇa*. The conclusion is that day is *prāṇa*. In the same way *sāyam* and *samāgāt* are played upon and *sāyam* (evening) is said to be *apāna*. *Prāṇa* and *prātar* fit together; not so *apāna* and *sāyam*. The whole is, therefore, valueless as to the translation of *prāṇa* and *apāna*.

(b) *Pravah*. This word occurs in ÇB. i. 4. 3. 3, where *āyāhi*, etc., is used with *apāna* and *bṛhacchocā* with *udāna*. The pun is plain only for the first two, viz.:—*pra* with *prāṇa* and *ā* with *apāna*. The reference is to the first *sāmidhenī*, which begins *pra vaḥ*, and to the second, which begins *Agna ā yāhi vītaye*. The identification of *prāṇa* with the first is a mere pun and indicates nothing as to its proper usage.

(c) *Prāñc*. The passage which we note is ÇB. x. 1. 4. 12. *Pratyañc* stands in contrast with *prāñc*, and the two breaths named in connection with these two words are *prāṇa* and *apāna*.

The important statements are:—(1) *Prāg devebhyo juhvati*, i. e. "They offer to the gods in front." (2) *Pratyañ manuṣyeṣv annaṁ dhīyate*, i. e., "Food is put in men in the reverse direction (or behind)." (3) Agni is the *prāṇa* of the gods and by *prāṇa* the gods eat food. (4) By *apāna* men eat food.

The proper interpretation of the passage is probably as follows: From in front men (priests) throw *ghi*, etc., upon the altar. The fire consumes the *ghi*. Now fire is the *prāṇa* of the gods, therefore the gods eat food by *prāṇa*. Hence Agni and *prāñ* and *prāṇa* go together. Again, the food which is the portion of the priests is eaten behind or to the west of the altar. *Apāna* has already been identified with the rear of the altar and is called *paçcāt prāṇa* in ÇB. viii. 1, 3, 6. May this not be all that is meant by saying that men eat food by *apāna?* There would seem to be a connection between this assertion and Āit. Up. i. 3, where *apāna* is called the "seizer of food." The fancy of the writer seems to have passed from the fact of men eating food at the *apāna* end of the altar to the conception of *apāna* as "seizer of food." It must be acknowledged that the passive statement, "Food is placed in men behind" is a very awkward way of saying that men eat their portion of food to the rear of the altar.

But while we may not insist on every point in this suggested interpretation, it may be insisted—as important for our purpose—that fire in consuming the food of the gods, i. e. *ghi*, etc., takes in what is thrown upon it, and therefore Eggeling's translation of *prāṇa* by "out-breathing" should not be allowed to stand.

(d) *Parāñc.* This word occurs with *prāṇa* in the Soma Graha chapters, already noticed, viz.: ÇB. iv. 1. 1 and iv. 1. 2. The contrasted word which goes with *udāna* is *pratyañc.* The usual word with *pratyañc* is *prāñc. Parāñc* is near enough, however, according to Hindu standards, to serve as a link with *pra* of *prāṇa.* We have already seen that *prāṇa* when with *udāna* assuredly cannot mean "out-breathing." The context, too, is decisive against such a translation. ÇB. iv. 1. 2. 27 concludes the chapter in which Soma Grahas and the three breaths are manipulated together. The section contains a sort of résumé in which *prāṇa* (i. e. *upāñçu*) is identified with the earth; *udāna* (i. e. *antaryāma*) with the sky; and *vyāna* (i. e. *upāñçu-savana*) with the atmosphere. A corresponding participle and verb are used with the name of each breath, viz.: *prāṇann abhiprāṇiti, udānann abhyudaniti,* and *vyānann abhivyaniti.* Each verb is followed by an accusative (1) *imām* (*pṛthivīm*), (2) *amuṁ lokam,* (3) *antarikṣam.* These accusatives are governed in each instance by the verb with which they stand. We may translate, as follows:

1. Breathing in, he breathes in towards this (earth).
2. Breathing up, he breathes upon that world.
3. Breathing pervasively, he pervades the atmosphere.

While the translation under 3 is only tentative, the contrast between *prāṇat* and *udānat* and the connection of earth with the former and sky with the latter emphatically suggests that *prāṇat* refers to the movement of breath from the mouth downward.

The identification of *vyāna* with the atmosphere is not without suggestion of a breath which is central and pervasive. Its central character is symbolized also in its correlation with the press-stone which in the Soma-pressing was placed between two vessels holding the Soma. Here may be recalled the conception of Ch. Up. i. 3. 5, according to which *vyāna* is the breath which abides when there is neither *prāṇa* nor *apāna.*

ÇB. ii. 2. 2. 15 is a passage which may not be passed over without notice. The preceding context refers to the immortal element, *agni,* being put by the gods within their own selves (*antarātmā*). Then in section 15 we have a description of the placing of the same immortal element in the individual man in connection with the churning out of fire from wood. Two compound verbs occur, i. e. *abhiprāṇiti* and *punar apāniti.* Eggeling translates, "to breathe upon" and "to again draw in breath." This is a misconception. The statement is that when fire is produced it is inhaled, for breath is fire (*taj jātam abhiprāṇ iti prāṇo vā agniḥ*). Further the writer adds, "He causes that which is thus produced (i. e. *agni*) to become that which is" (i. e. *prāṇa*),—*jātam evai 'nam etat santaṁ janayati.* Again the statement is added, *sa punar apāniti.* This, instead of meaning, "he again draws in breath," signifies the exact opposite, viz.: "he again (or, in turn) expels breath." Exhalation must follow inhalation and both processes are needed to make the establishment of *agni* (i. e. *prāṇa*) within the organism (*antarātmā*) complete. There is a still further objection to Eggeling's view. The main assertion of the section is that *prāṇa* is *agni.* Now in breathing the *vital* act is certainly inhalation. The divine Agni is very frequently, in the literature, called *āyus* (life), and it is, therefore, impossible to identify the non-vital act of exhalation with fire as Eggeling's translation would demand.

This review of salient passages from the ÇB. may be thus summed up:

1. *Prāṇa* is "in-breathing."

2. *Udāna* is "up- or out-breathing."

3. *Apāna* is used in two senses, (a) "Out-breathing; (b) The breath which is in the hinder part or lower part of the body. The meaning under (b) is further specialized so that *apāna* comes to be equivalent to *paçcāt prāṇa*, i. e., the anus.

4. There is nothing entirely decisive regarding *vyāna*, but the central pervading, always abiding breath is plainly suggested.

5. The location of *samāna* in the centre of the Fire-altar, which centre corresponds to the navel-region, furnishes a clear basis for the Upaniṣad definitions which have been dealt with above.

III. The Prāṇa-Series in the Upaniṣads.

The material arranges itself in two main divisions.

1. Passages in which explanations are attempted. These have already been dealt with and definite results obtained.

These results, when compared with the conclusions just now drawn from our scrutiny of the ÇB., justify the important inference that the basis of these explanations is to be found in the conceptions which took shape in connection with the building of the Sacrifice and of the Fire-altar. There are additions and developments, but the beginnings of all systematic explanations by Hindu writers are found in the ÇB.

2. Passages where the breaths are referred to in a symbolical way as quotations from or echoes of ritualistic formulas.

As we have already found in the ÇB. the ground-elements of the various Hindu explanations of the Prāṇa-Series, we are here especially interested in the question of the proper translation of the terms, notably of the first two. This question is of so much importance that a review of all the passages with a more or less detailed criticism of each seems advisable.

(1) *Prāṇāpānāu*, cf. Bṛh. Ār. Up. vi. 4. 12; Tāitt. Up. iii. 10. 2; Muṇḍ. Up. ii. 17; Ch. Up. i. 3. 3; Saṁnyāsa Up. iv.; and three Gītā instances.

In every instance, the compound seems to us to mean precisely the same as it does in the AV., viz.: "in-breathing and out-breathing." Deussen, however, translates the second, fourth and fifth instances by "Aushauch und Einhauch," and the first by "Ausatmung und Einatmung. In Muṇḍ. Up. ii. 17, on the other hand, he gives "Einhauch und Aushauch," doubtless because he finds there a clear reference to AV. xi. 4. 13. He should also have noted that Bṛh. Ār. Up. 4, 12 is a regular Atharva-like sorcery practice against a rival wife. His translation of this last passage seems all the more strange because in the two preceding sections, i. e., vi. 4. 10 and 11, he correctly translates *abhiprāṇyā 'pānyāt* and *apānyā 'bhiprāṇyāt* by "Erst einatmen, dann ausatmen," and "Erst ausatmen, dann einatmen."

In Tāitt. Up. iii. 10, the compound appears without any distinctive note of meaning and the earlier translation should be followed unless good reasons for the contrary be forthcoming.

Ch. Up. i. 3. 3 makes *vyāna* the bond of union (*saṁdhi*) between *prāṇa* and *apāna*. Assuredly in such a case the vital act of in-breathing is thought of first. To reverse the order, as Deussen *et al.* do, seems to us without justification. The section contains also the verbs *prāṇiti* and *apāniti* and in the context we find the negative participle of each form. The verbs, the participles, and the dual compound must all, of course, be translated in consonance with each other. There is no indication that the compound has lost its earlier meaning and, therefore, in all the forms *prāṇa* should be interpreted as "in-breathing" and *apāna* as "out-breathing."

Attention to the fanciful identification of *prāṇa* and *ud* of the word *udgītha* supplies a valuable hint as to the true interpretation. The statement is made that a man stands up by *prāṇa* (*prāṇena hy uttiṣṭhati*). This is plain reference to the simple phenomenon which any one may observe, that a man, who has been seated or lying down, instinctively draws in breath before or while rising. Hence *prāṇa* is inhalation.

The Saṁnyāsa Up. passage is immediately followed by a reference to *apāna* as the navel or possibly the anus. If this has any bearing upon the interpretation of the compound—an extremely doubtful supposition, since the compound is in a prose passage and *apāna* in a quoted stanza—its influence is certainly not in the direction of making *apāna* mean "Einhauch," as Deussen does.

(2) In Āit. Up. i. 4; ii. 4; iii. 4, *prāṇa* means either breath in general or in-breathing. Müller's translation of the word by "scent" is much too narrow an application of it—a restriction into which he was doubtless led by the connection of *prāṇa* with the nose. Since, however, the *prāṇa* which arises from the nose gives rise in turn to wind, the meaning is certainly not to be restricted to a subordinate function of the breath. Vāyu is everywhere correlated with the entire breath activity, i. e., with breath in general.

(3) Ch. Up. iii. 13 (cf. ÇB. viii. 1. 3. 6). This reference has already been noted. The full list of names is used and they are correlated with the various directions. In the matter of translation, Deussen rightly perceives that *prāṇa* means "Einhauch," not "Aushauch." Müller still holds to *prāṇa* and *apāna* as "up- and down-breathing." This is manifestly not accurate. Perhaps in such a passage translation of the terms is not to be attempted. It would probably be no more correct to say that *prāṇa* and *apāna* mean "in-breathing and out-breathing" than to use Müller's rendering. The basis of the symbolism is the bird-like fire-altar, in which the breath is conceived of as moving backward and forward. The forward breath (*prāñ prāṇa*) includes both in-breathing and out-breathing, and the backward breath (*pratyañ apāna*), all breath movements to the rear of the centre. As already intimated, it is probably best to merely transliterate the words. Deussen attempts a translation, but his effort can scarcely be deemed successful. His rendering of *samāna* by "Allhauch" has no induction of facts upon which to rest.

(4) Ch. Up. v. 19–23. This epochal passage sets forth the high Upaniṣad doctrine that inasmuch as the individual soul is not different from the Universal Self (*ātmā vāiçvānaraḥ;* cf. v. 18),

therefore the sage who recognizes this fact performs the whole vast ritual whenever he eats. All he needs to do is to say with the first mouthful of food, *prāṇāya svāhā*, and with the others in turn *vyānāya*, *apānāya*, *samānāya* and *udānāya svāhā*. The order of the names is the same as in Ch. Up. iii. 13, and we here recognize an oft-repeated formula; cf. Bloomfield's Concordance under "*Prāṇa*." As in iii. 13, Deussen translates the terms by Einhauch, Zwischenhauch, Aushauch, Allhauch and Aufhauch. Müller again has for *prāṇa* and *apāna* "up- and down-breathing." This can only be admitted if "up-breathing" refers to both inhalation and exhalation, and "down-breathing" to the breath movements below or back of the middle of the body.

The fact that *prāṇa* is said to satisfy[1] heaven, and *apāna* earth, might suggest this. This is not, however, what Müller means by "down-breathing," and his translation must be rejected.

Note that *vyāna* is said to satisfy the quarters. This may be taken, as illustrative of its meaning, as "breath everywhere diffused;" cf. ÇB. iv. 1. 2. 27.

(5) Prāṇāg. Up. i. sets forth doctrine similar to that which has just been alluded to. The mantra used in Ch. Up. v. 19–23 is repeated. *Prāṇa* is called the head or chief (*pradhāna*). The performer of the Prāṇāgnihotra offers water,

(a) In *prāṇa* with the little finger and thumb.
(b) In *apāna* with the nameless (*anāmikā*) or ring-finger.
(c) In *vyāna* with the middle finger.
(d) In *samāna* with the index finger.
(e) In *udāna* with all fingers.

This passage throws no new light upon the question of translation. It is impossible, as regards *apāna*, to determine whether it means "out-breathing" or intestinal breath movements, or is a mere name to fill out a formula. The supreme place given to *prāṇa*, however, makes it certain that it is either life-breath in general or in-breathing in particular. Such passages place a heavy burden of proof upon any one who would attempt to show that *apāna* can ever mean the vital act of inhalation.

In the sentence which follows the statement quoted above, it is interesting to note what is done with the water which the offerer takes on the various fingers. With the thumb and little finger he sprinkles water once upon the One Ṛṣi (*ekarṣi*) i. e. the sun or

---

[1] In AV. xiii. 3. 4, *prāṇa* is said to satisfy both heaven and earth.

fire; cf. esp. Muṇḍ. Up. iii. 2. 11; Praçna Up. ii. 11, and Bṛh. Ār. Up. v. 15. 1; with the nameless finger he sprinkles water twice on the Āhavanīya Fire, which is in the mouth (Garbha Up. iv; Māitri, vi. 36); with the middle finger he sprinkles water once in the Dakṣiṇa Fire, which is in the heart (Garbha Up. iv.); with the index finger he sprinkles water in the Gārhapatya Fire, which is in the belly (*udara*, cf. Garbha Up. iv.); with all the fingers he sprinkles water once in the all-atoning (*sarvaprāyaçcittīya*) Fire. This last fire is not mentioned in Garbha Up. The reference is probably to the organ of procreation. The Hindu holds that it is essential that every man should have a son in order to secure carrying out of the proper post mortem ceremonies. This may be the meaning here; cf. Āit. Brāh. vii. 13.

Probably in the word *ekarṣi* the eye is referred to, as it is frequently identified with the sun. It thus appears that five points or parts of the body are touched with water. As the abode of the Supreme Spirit, the body is the place of sacrifice.

(6) Māitri Up. vi. 9 uses the same mantra that we have noted under (4) and (5). Before beginning to eat, the knowing sacrificer clothes the *prāṇa* with water. This refers to the custom of rinsing the mouth before eating, which is to this day the common practice. By reason of this custom, water is called the clothing of *prāṇa* in Ch. Up. v. 2. 2. After *prāṇa* is clothed, the five mantras are repeated, doubtless each being accompanied with the taking of a morsel of food. The further explanation is added that the remainder is eaten in silence, and afterwards *prāṇa* is again clothed with water. As to translation, nothing new is developed.

(7) Bṛh. Ār. Up. i. 5. 3. The doctrine under discussion here is the affirmation that all forms of thought (*manas*), all forms of speech, and all forms of breath are varying manifestations of one Supreme Ātman. *Prāṇa*, *apāna*, *vyāna*, *udāna* and *samāna*, are all said to be *Ana*, i. e. *Prāṇa.* This statement is both a recognition that *ana* occurs in each of the names and that *prāṇa* (i. e. *ana*) is the generic entity of which the others are at most manifestations or forms. Now unless *prāṇa* is used in two different senses in the same sentence—an unlikely phenomenon—the first member of the series must express the vital act of inbreathing. Such considerations should have warned both Deussen and Müller that they were wrong in making *apāna* the vital act. In section 23 (34) of this same chapter, Deussen rightly

translates *prāṇyat* and *apānyāt* "by" einatmen and ausatmen," thus making his translation of the noun all the more inexplicable.

(8) Bṛh. Ār. Up. iii. 1. 10. *Prāṇa, apāna,* and *vyāna* are mentioned. They are described microcosmically (*adhyātmam*) as corresponding to the three hymns of praise accompanying the sacrifice, the invocatory, the sacrificial (uttered during the sacrifice), and the praising verse. Deussen here givés *prāṇa* and *apāna* their proper significance. Müller, however, has "up- and down-breathing" as usual. The symbolism which here connects *vyāna* with *yājya* is perhaps intended to bring out its abiding, continuous character; cf. Ch. Up. i. 3. 3 and 5.

(9) Bṛh Ār. Up. iii. 4. 1. The *Sarvāntaraḥ* (*ātmā*) functions in *prāṇa, apāna, vyāna, udāna* and *samāna.* Each noun is accompanied by its corresponding verb, i. e. *prāṇiti, apāniti, vyāniti, udāniti* and *samāniti.* Deussen rightly translates *prāṇa* by "Einhauch," and *apāna* by "Aushauch." If Müller's "down-breathing" for *apāna* could be understood as referring to breath movements below the navel, it might be admitted; he does not, however, seem to have attained to any such insight in connection with *apāna.*

Such a passage as this looks promising on the outside. Surely where both nouns and verbs are used we are coming to close quarters with the problem of translation and may expect definite and satisfactory results! On the contrary, almost no results are obtainable. We have here, in all probability, nothing more than an analogical filling out of the verb-series on the basis of *prāṇiti* and *apāniti* which have the definite meanings of "to breathe in" or "to breathe," and to "breathe out or off." √*An* with *ud* we have found in a few places with the meaning of "to breathe up;" cf. AV. iii. 13. 5; ÇB. iii. 8. 3. 32; iv. 1. 2. 27. √*An* with *vi* appears in AV. v. 2. 2, but yields there no meaning beyond that of the simple verb. Its occurrence in ÇB. iv. 1. 2. 37 and its correlation with the atmosphere have been noted above.

√*An* with *sam* occurs only in RV. x. 55. 5. Its force there gives no help here. Perhaps the strongest proof that *samāniti* is an analogical formation without special significance is to be found in the fact that in the later explanations of *samāna,* this verb is not used but instead a play is made upon *samāna* by using the root √*nī* with *sama* or with *sam* and *ā.* Deussen omits *samāniti* in his translation of this passage. Barring the first and second verbs and possibly the third, a similarly analogical character probably belongs to the other terms, and it is better, therefore, merely to transliterate.

(10) Bṛh. Ār. Up. iii. 9. 26. Here a series of questions and answers set forth the dependence of each member of the Prāṇa-Series upon the one immediately preceding it.

In what do *tvam* and *ātmā* find their support (*pratiṣṭhitāu*)? *Prāṇā.*

In what does *prāṇa* find its support (*pratiṣṭhitaḥ*)? *Apāna.*

In what does *apāna* find its support (*pratiṣṭhitaḥ*)? *Vyāna.*

In what does *vyāna* find its support (*pratiṣṭhitaḥ*)? *Udāna.*

In what does *udāna* find its support (*pratiṣṭhitaḥ*)? *Samāna.*

The passage is unique in its presentation, The kernel of it is in the first two members of the Series, i. e. "*tvam* and *ātmā*," and *prāṇa.* The statement amounts to an assertion that the continuance of individual consciousness and the permanence of the individual organism (Çaṅkara notes that *ātman* here means "body") depends upon *prāṇa.*

From this as a starting point, the author, moved by some fancy, passes on to an analogical completion of the series. He is not to be taken too seriously. The assertion, taken literally, is a direct contradiction of Bṛh. Ār. Up. i. 5. 3, where all are said to be forms of *prāṇa.* Here, on the contrary, *samāna* would seem to be the fountain and source of all, i. e., if we press the literal assertion. As already intimated, however, we are not to find anything here except a passion for analogical statement, and the main point is that *tvam* and *ātmā* depend upon *prāṇa.*

Deussen is wrong in returning to the meaning "Aushauch" for *prāṇa.* It is certainly inaccurate to speak of *tvam* and *ātmā* as depending upon the non-vital act of out-breathing. Müller recognizes the impossibility of his favorite "up-breathing" and translates by the general term "breath."

(11) Bṛh. Ār. Up. v. 14. 3. In this chapter the Gāyatrī verse is manipulated. Three words are sought which will make up the necessary eight syllables. These are *prāṇa, apāna, vyāna.*

Again in Tāitt. Up. i. 5. 3, *prāṇa, apāna* and *vyāna* are identified with the Vyāhṛtis, i. e. *bhūs, bhuvas,* and *svar.*

In neither of the above sections does the context throw any light upon the question of translation. Following, therefore, the results already gained, we hold that *prāṇa* and *apāna* mean "in-breathing" and "out-breathing," and not, as Deussen thinks, "Aushauch" and "Einhauch." *Vyāna* had best be left untouched.

(12) Tăitt. Up. i. 7. In correlation with the complete Prāṇa-Series, which is said to be treated microcosmically (*adhyātmam*), a series of both psychical and fleshly entities is brought forward, thus :

Prāṇa, *apāna*, *vyāna*, *udāna*, and *samāna*.
Eye, ear, *manas*, speech, and skin (i. e. touch, *tvac*).
Skin (*carma*), flesh, sinews, bone, and marrow.

Cf. also Ch. Up. iii. 13; v. 19–23; ÇB. viii. 1. 3. 6.

How thoroughly formulaic the Prāṇa-Series is, these correlations clearly show. If we translate even the first member, it must not be by "Aushauch," but by "Einhauch" instead.

(13) Tăitt. Up. ii. 2. This is the notable chapter in which man is described as consisting of a combination of various envelopes or coverings (*koçāḥ*), which are named respectively "food-made" (*annamaya*) ; "breath-made" (*prāṇamaya*) ; "thought-made" (*manomaya*); "knowledge-made" (*vijñānamaya*); and "bliss-made" (*ānandamaya*).

In section 2, the *prāṇamaya koça* is described as having the form of a man whose head is *prāṇa*, whose right side is *vyāna* and whose left side is *apāna;* cf. TĀ. viii. 2. Deussen gives to *prāṇa* its original meaning of "Einhauch." It is best in such a case to leave all the terms untranslated.

(14) Kaṭha Up. v. 3. This stanza is of great importance. The text runs :

> *ūrdhvam prāṇam unnayaty apānam pratyag asyati*
> *madhye vāmanam āsīnaṁ viçve devā upāsate,*

"He brings upward the upward *prāṇa* and throws *apāna* in the reverse direction. All the gods reverence the Dwarf seated in the middle (of the body)."

From the ÇB. we are prepared to understand that the *prāṇa* which moves upward includes both in- and out-breathing, while *pratyañ* with the verb √*as*, "to throw," describes the breath which passes down and out by the anus and sexual organ. Lack of adequate familiarity with the material of the ÇB. doubtless accounts for Deussen's note to the stanza, viz.:—"*Prāṇa* ist hier Aushauch, *apāna*, Einhauch; nicht (wie später) der Verdauungswind." On the contrary, *prāṇa* is not "Aushauch," nor is *apāna* "Einhauch." Further, while according to Āit. Up. i. 3 *apāna* has digestion as a part of its activity, we have not found it restricted to "Verdauungswind" either earlier or later.

However, in this same note Deussen gives his reason for holding to his translation. The concluding clause of his note runs thus, "Welches (i. e. *apāna* as Verdauungswind) bei der Wiederkehr in Vers 5 nicht passt." Now stanza 5 is as follows :

na prāṇena nā 'pānena martyo jīvati kaçcana
itareṇa tu jīvanti yasminn etāv upāçritāu,

"Not by *prāṇa*, nor by *apāna* does any mortal live;
But by another do they live in whom these two find their support."

Prāṇa and *apāna* undoubtedly mean "in-breathing and out-breathing" in conformity with the earlier and prevailing use of the two words. Deussen's mistake consists in assuming that stanza 5 rules in the interpretation of stanza 3. The phrase *etad vāi 'tat* which stands between stanzas 4 and 5, indicates that one phase of the subject is closed and another begins. This, therefore, does away with the supposed necessity of squaring stanza 3 with stanza 5, or vice versa.

These two stanzas, thus close together, furnish the classical example in the Upaniṣads of both the primitive and permanent use of *prāṇa* and *apāna* on the one hand; and, on the other hand, of that use whose development was made possible by the building of the living sacrifice and the animated Fire-altar—which use finds definite statement in Māitri, Amṛtabindu, and Praçna Upaniṣads, etc.

(15) In Māitri Up. vi. 5, *prāṇa*, *apāna* and *vyāna* are named as making up the breath-endowed (*prāṇavat*) form of Brahman. There is a degree of definiteness here which would seem to justify an attempt at translating *vyāna*. As in Ch. Up. i. 3. 3 and 5, it doubtless means the breath which abides in the body when the regular breath activity is quiescent—when there is neither *prāṇa* nor *apāna*.

(16) Māitri Up. vi. 33. Here the five members of the Prāṇa-Series are called the bricks of the fire to which *prāṇa* corresponds. By means of the bricks the (Āhavanīya) Fire is supplied with a head, two wings, a back, and a tail. The order of the names is *prāṇa, vyāna, apāna, samāna,* and *udāna*. The arrangement of these, if ÇB. viii. 1. 3. 6 be recalled, would give what the explanation implies, viz.:—a bird-like form, thus :

(3) *Apāna* (tail)	(2) *Vyāna* (wing) (4) *Samāna* (back) (5) *Udāna* (wing).	(1) *Prāṇa* (head)

If translation be attempted, *prāṇa* must be made to include both in-breathing and out-breathing; and *apāna*, the breath movements back of the centre of the body.

In Māitri Up. vii. 1–5, each section contains one of the above names and they appear in the same order as in vi. 33. A long list of other correlations accompanies each term. In both the above passages it is best to look upon the list of names as merely formulaic.

Observe that although in Māitri Up. ii. 6 (above, ch. II.) there is a serious attempt at an explanation of the various names of the Prāṇa-Series, that explanation seems to have no influence upon vi. 33 and vii. 1–5. This would argue for the composite character of the Upaniṣad.

(17) JB. Up. ii. 5. In this passage the names of the Prāṇa-Series are increased to six by the addition of *avāna*. There are two ways in which the rise of *avāna* may be accounted for:

1. It may be an analogical formation from the compound verb $\sqrt{an}$ with *ava* which appears, in the sense of the simple verb, in ÇB. iv. 3. 2. 6 and iv. 6. 1. 5.

2. It may be formed from the adverb *avāñc* which is frequently used in the ÇB. *Avāna* may stand for *avāñ prāṇa*. *Apāna* is, to be sure, the synonym of *avāñ prāṇa*. This fact would not, however, prevent another author from using the five names as a mere formula and adding another created from *avāñ prāṇa*.

It is to be observed that *apāna*, *vyāna*, *samāna*, *avāna*, and *udāna* are called "Sons of *prāṇa*." *Prāṇa* thus holds the supreme place and must either mean breath in general or inhalation.

(18) JB. Up. ii. 22. Following upon a series of psycho-physical correlations between (a) Speech and Agni; (b) Manas and Moon; (c) Sight and Sun; (d) Hearing and Quarters, the statement is made that *apāna* is Bṛhaspati, and *prāṇa* is Prajāpati. *Apāna* is "lord of Speech" because in speaking breath is exhaled. *Prāṇa* is "lord of offspring" because it is "rich in sons," cf. ii. 5 above.

Oertel's translation by "exhalation" and "breath" is correct.

(19) JB. Up. iv. 22. This chapter contains both an attempt to define creation in terms of the Prāṇa-Series and also states the cosmical correlations of the various names. The correlations are, as below,

1. Prāṇa.........Sun. 2. Apāna.........Agni.
3. Vyāna........Waters. 4. Samāna........Quarters.
5. Udāna.........Moon.

We may note also the corresponding correlations in Ch. Up. iii. 13 and v. 19-23.

1. Prāṇa.........Sun. 2. Vyāna.........Moon.[1]
3. Apāna ....Agni. 4. Samāna........Parjanya.
5. Udāna.........Ākāça.

The description of creation starts with space or ether (*ākāça*). [Strictly *āçā*, Ed.] This became waters. The waters, as a result of practicing austerities (*tapas*) breathed out forward (*prācīḥ prāçvasan*), uttering the sound "huss." Thus arose (*abhavat*) *prāṇa*. Then these (waters), having breathed in (*prāṇya*), breathed out (*apānan*). Thus *apāna* arose. Upon this there follows a series of analogical statements accounting for each member of the Prāṇa-Series in turn, viz.: *apānya vyānan; vyānya samānan;* and *samānyo 'dānan.* These words recall the full series of nouns and verbs in Bṛh. Ār. Up. iii. 4. 1, and seem to invite translation. Though spoken of the primeval waters, the reference to real or supposed breath activities in man is undoubted. But careful scrutiny soon creates a suspicion that the three last verbs are mere formula-filling words, made for the occasion. Whence comes the long *ā* after *vi*, *sam* and *ud?* Whitney, to be sure, in his "Roots and Verb-Forms" gives the form in long *ā*, but may he not have used this or a similar passage as the basis of the form? It is probable that the *ā* comes by analogy from the *ā* of *prāṇiti* and *apāniti*, and any attempt at translation is likely to be wasted labor. The results of the labor which we have expended are too meagre and uncertain to justify putting them on record. The first two terms of the series are of importance because they seem to Deussen to furnish an argument for his translation of *prāṇa* and *apāna* as "Aushauch"

---

[1] Moon and waters are in effect the same cosmic thing.

and "Einhauch;" cf. Gesch. der Phil., vol. i., pt. ii., page 250. Neither do we here agree with him. The *prāṇa* which arose when the waters, uttering the "huss," breathed out forward, was breath in general apart from any distinction as to in- and out-breathing. *Pra* in *prācīḥ* and *prāçvasan* creates the opportunity to make a pun upon *prāṇa*, but the question of the direction of the breath movement is not yet raised.[1] The entire first statement which describes how *prāṇa* arose from heated water amounts to saying, what appears again and again in the literature, that heat and breath are identical.

In the second statement, the waters, from which breath in general has been produced, are said to experience the ordinary breath activities. By means of generic breath, inhalation takes place and this is, of course, followed by exhalation. This is precisely what we should expect and thus *prāṇya* and *apānan* retain their ordinary and proper significance.

Breath and Scent.

(20) We now come to the consideration of a number of passages of great importance for the interpretation of *prāṇa* and *apāna*, especially the latter. The list includes the references upon which Deussen rests his case for the translation which we have already had such frequent occasion to controvert in the passages reviewed above.

The references to be brought under discussion are with three exceptions found in the Upaniṣads. They are as follows:

AV. xix. 60. 1 (cf. Vāit. Sūtra iii. 14); Kāuṣ. Up. iii. 4, 6, 7; VS. xxv. 2; Pāras. Gṛh. Sūtra i. 19. 4; Praṇava Up. i. (cf. GB. i. 1, 18); JB. Up. iv. 26; i. 60. 5; ii. 1. 16 and 19; ii. 10; Ch. Up. i. 2. 2; Bṛh. Ār. Up. i. 3. 3; iii. 2. 2.

In AV. xix. 60. 1, the location of *prāṇa* is said to be in the nostrils, *Vāñ ma āsan nasoḥ prāṇaç cakṣur akṣṇoḥ çrotraṁ karṇayoḥ.*

In Praṇava Up. i., *prāṇa*, nostrils, scent and smelling appear together in symbolic correlation with the *u* sound of the syllable

[1] [This is, at least, doubtful, in view of the juxtaposition. "Thus arose" (in the translation) rather dims the original connection (*huss ity eva prācīḥ prāçvasan ; sa vāva prāṇo 'bhavat*): The hissing, *huss*, waters breathed forth forward and that (forth forward breathing) became *prāṇa*.—Ed.]

4

Om. Cf. also ÇB. xii. 9. 1. 14; xiv. 3. 2. 17, where the nostrils are called "the path of *prāṇa.*"

The statement that odors are known by *prāṇa* (*prāṇena gandhān veda*) is found in JB. Up. iv. 26; cf. ÇB. x. 5. 2. 15.

Kāuṣ. Up. iii. 4, 6, 7, has the following very definite assertions: *Prāṇena sarvān gandhān āpnoti. Prāṇo gandhaṁ kiṁcana prajñāpayet. Prāṇa eva 'smin sarve gandhā abhivisṛjyante.*

On the other hand, in VS. xxv. 2, the nostrils are especially correlated with *apāna*. Further in Pāras. Gṛh. Sūtra i. 19. 4, food is said to be obtained by *prāṇa* (cf. ÇB. xii. 9. 1. 14, and note by contrast Āit. Up. i. 3. 4), and scent by *apāna*. In this latter passage the distinction is doubtless between breath in the mouth and breath in the nose. But even so, the two last references ascribe to *apāna* a function which according to all the other quotations belongs to *prāṇa*, and this change is both to be understood and accounted for.

In order to the solution of this problem, we may first bring under review those of the remaining listed passages which occur in descriptions of the famous contest between Devas and Asuras. JB. Up. i. 60. 5, runs as follows: *te 'pāneno 'dagāyan; taṁ tathāi 'vā 'kurvan; tasmād bahu kiṁca kiṁcā 'pānena jighrati, surabhi cāi 'nena jighrati durgandhi ca.* When the gods sang the Udgītha with *apāna*, the Asuras were able to mix it with evil, hence it is described as the agent in smelling both pleasant and unpleasant odors. JB. Up. ii. 1. 16 contributes the following to the treatment of *apāna:*

tam pāpmā 'nvasṛjyata; sa yad evā 'pānena pāpaṁ gandham apāniti, sa eva sa pāpmā.

In verse 15, *apāna* is said to be the Udgātar. Whatever it breathes out by *apāna* (*apānena apāniti*), that it sang to itself; but the other desires, whatever they are, those it sang to the gods (*atha ya itare kāmās tān devebhyaḥ.*) Following this comes the statement of verse 16, quoted above, that evil was created along with it (*apāna*) and that the evil referred to is the evil smell which he (any one) exhales with exhalation.

JB. Up. ii. 1. 19 is a declaration that when *prāṇa* is used as Udgātar evil is not created, and that therefore, by this *prāṇa* one neither speaks evil, nor thinks evil, nor sees evil, nor exhales an evil odor (*na pāpāṁ gandham apāniti*).

With reference to JB. Up. ii. 10.; Ch. Up. i. 2, and Bṛh. Ār. Up. i. 3, the points to be noted are the following:

(a) In JBU. and Bṛ. Ār. Up., *apāna* is not named, but *prāṇa* is said to be affected by evil, while *mukhya prāṇa* alone escapes, otherwise *āsanya prāṇa*. JBU. ii. 10. 17 closes with these words, *sa yad eva prāṇena (pāpām) prāṇiti, sa eva sa pāpmā*. Bṛ. Ār. Up., i. 3. 3 closes thus, *sa yaḥ sa pāpmā yad eve 'dam apratirūpaṁ jighrati sa eva sa pāpmā*.

(b) In Ch. Up. i. 2, *nāsikya prāṇa* is contaminated by the Asuras, while *mukhya prāṇa* alone escapes. Verse 2 ends with the statement which, with some changes and additions, is quoted at JBU. i. 60. 5, i. e., *tasmāt teno 'bhayaṁ jighrati surabhi ca durgandhi ca*.

The plain inference from a comparison of all these Deva-Asura passages is that *apāna*, *nāsikya prāṇa* and even *prāṇa* are used synonymously. Since the last two clearly refer to the nasal breath in general without reference to the direction of its movement, we are justified in interpreting *apāna* in the same way. The stereotyped character of the Deva-Asura fable leaves no alternative here.

It is impossible to say with Deussen that *apāna* means "Einhauch" and *prāṇa* "Aushauch," for that would be to make the activity unassailable by the Asuras a non-vital one. Moreover, an attempt to get out of the "frying pan" of difficulty by translating *apāna* and *apāniti* in JBU. ii. 1. 16 by "in-breathing" and "inhales" would at once involve a fall into the "fire" of JBU. ii. 10. 17, where in a similar context it would be meaningless to translate *prāṇa* and *prāṇiti* by "out-breathing" and "exhales."

In JBU. i. 60. 5, therefore, we take *apāna* to mean the entire nasal breath-activity. The way in which *apāna* came to take the place of *nāsikya prāṇa* may have been as follows:

1. The effect of the victory of the Asuras over the Devas in the matter of the nasal breath was that evil odors, as well as pleasant, came to be perceived thereby.

2. From the anus evil odors are frequently emitted.

3. *Apāna* is shown by the ÇB. and the Upaniṣads to have been regularly used to describe both the anus and the breath which issues from it.

4. By means of the nasal breath the odors from the *apāna*-anus are perceived, as well as all other evil odors.

5. This suggestion of identity between the nasal breath and that which issues from the anus seems to the author of JBU. a

sufficient ground for putting *apāna* in the place of *nāsikya prāṇa* in the fable which he quotes from the Ch. Up.

In JBU. ii. 1. 15–16, these two ideas of *apāna*, i. e. as nasal breath and anus breath, are definitely brought together. *Apāna* as Udgātar is doubtless the nasal breath. When, however, the words *apānena papaṁ gandham apāniti* are used, the reference is undoubtedly to the exhalation of evil odors from the anus. Observe that below, in verse 19, it is said that one does not exhale an evil odor by *prāṇa: prāṇena na pāpaṁ gandham apāniti.*

Not only does this clearly explain how *apāna* came to be given the place of *nāsikya prāṇa* in the Deva-Asura controversy, but we have at the same time come upon the origin of that misunderstanding on the basis of which some later Hindu authorities have taken *apāna* as meaning "out-breathing." That the word is so taken, we have never meant to deny. What we do deny is that it has such a meaning in the material which we have been reviewing. We dissent from Deussen in all his Upaniṣad passages, including JBU. i. 60. 5. There is clear evidence, however, that Hindu writers of a later time did give that meaning to *apāna* which Deussen attempts to apply to a portion of the references in his "Sechzig Upanishads."

E. g., Çaṅkara in his commentary on the Vedānta Sūtras takes this position; cf. Appendix. Further, Rudradatta on Āpast. Çr. Sūtra xiii. 8. 6, says *prāṇatā bahirgamitavāyunā; apānatā pratyāhṛtavāyunā.* Quoted by Böhtlingk through Caland; cf. Sächs. Ges. Wiss. 1897, p. 120.

Eggeling (SBE. vol. xliii. p. 15), to the same purpose, quotes Sāyaṇa on Tāitt. S. iv. 3. 3, as explaining *prāṇa* by *bahiḥ sañcārarūpa*, and *apāna* by *punar antaḥ sañcārarūpa.*

To this list belongs also Pāras. Gṛh. Sūtra i. 19. 4, noted above. The origin of this later opinion that *apāna* means "out-breathing" is probably, as already intimated, to be found in the phrase, *apānena pāpaṁ gandham apāniti* (JBU. ii. 1. 16). The meaning, as has been shown, points to the exhalation of bad odor from the anus. The context is, however, such as to readily suggest another interpretation. In sentences which immediately precede, various psychical activities are referred to in a way to suggest by analogy that *pāpaṁ gandham apāniti* applies to the "receiving" of evil odors; cf. *cakṣuṣā paçyati* in verse 10 and *çrotreṇa çṛṇoti* in verse 13.

Here, then, is the starting point of a misconception which was followed by Çaṅkara *et al.*, and has beset the pathway of modern translators in their handling of the older material.

Oertel suggested on page 236 of his translation of JBU. (JAOS. xvi.), that such a passage as ii. 1. 16 might be looked upon as a key to the use of *apāna* as "in-breathing." I am further greatly indebted to him for an illuminating statement of his position in a personal letter.

Deussen (Gesch. der Phil., vol. i, pt. ii, p. 250) criticises him in the interests of his own view that *apāna* means "in-breathing" in JBU. i. 60. 5, and ii. 1. 16. The criticism of the latter passage is without force because it rests upon a misconception of the whole situation. The criticism of the former reference has some force as against the word "exhalation," which Oertel uses as a translator, not as an interpreter. This criticism falls to the ground when *apāna* is recognized as the equivalent of *nāsikya prāṇa*.

For Böhtlingk's position, which is of dissent from Deussen, cf. Ber. Gesell. der Wiss., Phil-Hist. Classe, 1897, pp. 80 ff. and 129.

There remains the important reference in Bṛh. Ār. Up. iii. 2, upon which Deussen places great emphasis as justifying his translation of *prāṇa* and *apāna* as "Aushauch" and "Einhauch."

Both the Mādhyaṁdina and Kāṇva Recensions have:

Prāṇo vai grahaḥ so 'pānenā 'tigraheṇa gṛhīto 'pānena hi gandhāñ jighrati. Böhtlingk suggests that the line should read: *Prāṇo vai grahaḥ; sa gandhenā 'tigraheṇa gṛhītaḥ prāṇena hi gandhāñ jighrati.* These emendations bring the assertion here made into exact analogy with the seven similar statements which follow after.

In each case the psychical organ, which is named in the first part of each explanation as a *graha* (fetter), appears in the concluding part in the instrumental case. The first statement alone, in the form in which it has come to us, is an exception to this analogy, and, therefore, Böhtlingk's emendation carries a good deal of force. If the text is to be changed, he is clearly right. But had the text been looked upon as impossible, surely one of the standard texts would have remedied it. While, therefore, we consider Böhtlingk's emendation to be valuable as a suggestion, we would not base an argument against Deussen's position upon it.

On the other hand, however, the text as it stands cannot be claimed for Deussen's position and may be interpreted against it.

1. The eight statements deal with sense organs and their objects (i. e. *atigrahas* or *viṣayas*). No other passage has yet come to light in which *apāna* is described as the *viṣaya* of *prāṇa.* Scents, however, are frequently stated to be the *viṣaya* of *prāṇa.*

2. The analogy of the first statement with the seven which follow breaks down in two ways.

(a) The instrumental case of *prāṇa* should appear in the closing sentence. This has been referred to above.

(b) The analogy demands that the first *apānena* should mean the same as *gandhān* at the close.

We have noted above that in one instance at least *apāna* stands in the place of *nāsikya prāṇa* and even *prāṇa* as breath in the nose. Since the *prāṇa* which begins the statement probably refers to the breath in the nose, the demand of analogy would be fulfilled, if this meaning be given to the final *apānena.*

In the same way the correlation between *apāna* and scent, to which reference has already been made, may satisfy the demands of analogy in the matter of (b) above.

3. The whole series of statements assumes that the "*atigrahas*" are properties of external things. The only sense in which *apāna* can be so described, is as scent itself or as exhalation from those objects which possess odor as a property. Shall we not then say that the first *apānena* really means "scent"? Thus the demands of analogy (b) are satisfied.

There are, then, two alternatives for the interpretation of this passage, since Deussen's translation of *prāṇa* by "out-breathing" has no support at the era of this Upaniṣad.

(1) The text has been changed in the interests of a later view and Böhtlingk's emendation is to be adopted.

(2) *Apāna* is used in the two senses of "nasal breath" and "scent." According to the first it is synonymous with *prāṇa* (cf. Deva--Asura passages) and satisfies analogy (a). According to the second it is synonymous with *gandhān* and satisfies analogy (b).

IV. The Prāṇa-Series in GB.; TĀ.; and the Sūtras.

The material has already been summarized above. No detailed discussion is necessary. A cursory reading of the passages will deepen the impression already made that the five names are merely formulaic, and in ordinary—that is to say not universal—usage carried to the mind of the hearer concrete conceptions of separate breath processes, i. e. were untranslatable. As especially effective in strengthening this impression may be noted:

1. The double plurals in GB. i. 2. 5; i. 2. 16 (cf. AV. xv. 15 and 16), and i. 1. 39, where fifteen *prāṇas, apānas, vyānas, samānas* and *udānas;* seven *prāṇas* and *apānas;* and seven *prāṇas, apānas,* and *vyānas* are respectively assumed.

2. The triplet of dual compounds, i. e. *prāṇāpānāu, samānavyānāu,* and *udānarūpe;* cf. GB. i. 3. 13; ii. 1. 7; Vāit. Sūtra iii. 20, and Kāuç. Sūtra lxii. 4.

Résumé of Results.

The purpose of the review just closed has been to ascertain the origin, and estimate the value, of the Hindu explanations of the Prāṇa-Series; at the same time to grapple with the question of the proper interpretation and translation of the various terms.

Our conclusions may be summarized as follows:

1. The starting point of the Prāṇa-Series is the word *prāṇa,* i. e. breath in general.

2. The division of the breath activity into in- and out-breathing is primitive and appears in the early literature in the crystallized dual compound, *prāṇāpānāu.*

3. With his habit of careful observation, the Hindu may, and in all probability did early take note of the interval between respirations. This led him to the assumption of an abiding breath whose influence remained even in the absence of *prāṇa* and *apāna,* hence the name *vyāna,* i. e. "breathing apart."

4. A powerful inclination to symbolism marks even the earliest records of the Hindus. It is not strange that *prāṇa* and *apāna* were early drafted into service. As long as but two or three entities were to be symbolically handled, *prāṇa* and *apāna,* or *prāṇa, apāna,* and *vyāna* were sufficient. It is easy to conceive that in a reign of symbolism these names would become favorites and a demand would soon arise for other similar terms. The verb $\sqrt{an}$ was early known with *sam* (RV. x. 55. 5), and *ud* (AV. iii. 13. 4), as well as with *pra, apa* and *vi.*

The demand was therefore met by forming nouns from these verbs also, the *a* being lengthened to *ā* after the analogy of *prāṇa* and *apāna.*

The lengthened vowel of *vyāna* would indicate for it a similar origin. While we think that this is most probable, we are not, as intimated above, unwilling to admit that it may have had an empiric origin.

5. The five words thus formed gradually came to hold an important place in the current symbolism. The use of the terms as a formula opened up the way for a change in meaning of *apāna* by first weakening the sense of its empiric use and then giving its place to *udāna*, doubtless because it seemed etymologically better suited than *apāna* to express the idea of "out-breathing." Accordingly *prāṇodānāu* plays a large role in ÇB. to the exclusion of *prāṇāpānāu*.

6. In connection with the building of the Fire-altar or the Sacrificer into which it was necessary to put life, it was found convenient and fitting to identify the different members of the Series with the bricks used in the various parts of the structure. Indeed, it was probably this demand which motived the rise of *prāṇodānāu* by calling for a different use of *apāna*.

7. The presence of these words, sometimes five, sometimes less, could not fail to provoke attempts at explanation. These attempts are recorded in the Upaniṣads and are based, to some extent at least, if not wholly, upon the way the Series is handled in the ÇB.

For example, the location of *apāna* in the tail of the bird-like altar prepared the way for its location in the lower intestine and the urinary passage; the locating of *samāna* in the middle formed a good starting point for identifying it with the process of digestion; and the use of *udāna* for "out-breathing" gave a point of departure for the assertion that the soul leaves the body by *udāna* (Praçna Up. iii.).

8. These definitions and other later ones (cf. Appendix) are more or less interesting contributions to Hindu ideas of anatomy and physiology, but have no value in themselves, since they do not account for the formation of the Prāṇa-Series on an empiric basis. Each attempted explanation is to be taken, in so far as it is not merely traditional, as the expression of an individual opinion.

9. In the matter of translation our results are mainly negative. Where the full series occurs, it is always symbolical and nothing more than transliteration should be attempted, even in these most appealing instances where each term is accompanied by its verb.

10. One positive result, however, of no inconsiderable value, has been reached—a result in itself important enough to justify the investigation which has been carried on, viz:—We have found that *prāṇa*, in all cases where breath processes are referred to,

means either the double process of inhalation, or "in-breathing" as contrasted with "out-breathing."

We have also lighted upon the probable origin of the misconstruction which led to the inversion, by some writers, of the early and proper meaning of *prāṇa* and *apāna.*

This result will require the modification of the *prāṇa* passages in those current translations which read the later and misconceived meaning into the earlier literature; and will, we trust, be of real service to those who in the future shall have occasion to handle the members of the Prāṇa-Series.

APPENDIX.

Later Definitions.

The Prāṇa-Series does not form an integral part of the Vedānta and Sāṁkhya Sūtras. Commentators have, however, given expression to their views.

I. Commentary to the Vedānta Sūtras.

Çaṅkara in his commentary to the Vedānta Sūtras (ii. 4, 12) gives the following definitions:

(1) *Prāṇa* is the breath whose course is forward and whose function is exhalation, etc. *Prāgvṛttir ucchvāsādikarmā.*

(2) *Apāna* is the breath whose course is downward and whose function is inhalation, etc. *Avāgvṛttir niçvāsādikarmā.*

(3) *Vyāna* is the breath which functions in the junction of these two (*prāṇa* and *apāna*) and is the cause of powerful activities (Ch. Up. i. 3. 5). *Tayoḥ saṁdhāu vartamāno vīryavatkarmahetuḥ.*

(4) *Udāna* is the breath whose course is upward and which is the cause of departure, etc. *Ūrdhvavṛttir utkrāntyādihetuḥ.*

(5) *Samāna* is the breath which leads the juices of food to equality (i. e. assimilates them) in all the members.

Great though the name of Çaṅkara be, he has misconceived his material, and the error of some modern translators has been in following his lead.

2. The Vedāntasāra.

(Khāṇḍa 13 of Text; cf. Jacob's Manual of Hindu Pantheism.)

(1) *Prāṇa* is the breath which goes forward and has the tip of the nose as its place of activity.

(2) *Apāna* is the breath which goes downward and has the anus, etc., as its place of activity.

(3) *Vyāna* is the breath which goes in all directions and has the entire body as its place of activity.

(4) *Udāna* is the breath which has its place in the throat, goes upward, and is the (from life) departing wind.

(5) *Samāna* is the breath which produces the assimilation of that food, etc., which having been eaten and drunk, has gone into the midst of the body.

Observe that our author has an adequate conception of the facts as to *prāṇa* and *apāna*, as transmitted through the ÇB. The other definitions are also familiar.

It may not be out of place to note that our investigation was completed before we knew the position of the Vedāntasāra. We would, therefore, strongly commend the insight of our author as against Çañkara !

Five other winds (*vāyavaḥ*) are also mentioned and described:

1. *Nāga* produces vomiting.
2. *Kūrma* produces winking.
3. *Kṛkala* produces sneezing.
4. *Devadatta* produces yawning.
5. *Dhanaṁjayaḥ* produces enlargement.

For an allusion to these "breaths" and four others, cf. Sarv. Up. 10.

3. Gāuḍapāda's Commentary to the Sāñkhya Sūtras.

(Cf. Davies, Hindu Philosophy, p. 66.)

(1) *Prāṇa* is inspiration and expiration.

(2) *Apāna* is the breath functioning in the lower parts of the body.

(3) *Samāna* is the breath which conducts the food, etc., equally through the body.

(4) *Udāna* is the vital force which causes the pulsations of the arteries in the upper part of the body from the navel to the head.

(5) *Vyāna* is the breath by which internal divisions and diffusion through the body are effected.

4. Sāñkhya-tattva Kāumudī.

(Kārikā 29; cf. R. Garbe's Sāñkhya Phil., p. 256.)

(1) *Prāṇa* is the breath whose place of activity is from the point of the nose through the heart and navel to the great toe.

(2) *Apāna* is the breath whose place of activity is in the neck, the back, the anus (whence it escapes), the genitals and the ribs.

(3) *Samāna* is the breath whose place of activity is in the heart, the navel, and all the joints.

(4) *Udāna* is the breath whose place of activity is in the heart, the neck, the palate, the brain-pan and below the eye-brows.

(5) *Vyāna* is the breath whose place of activity is in the skin. Cf. here the PW. "It is the principle which mediates the circulation of juices and puts sweat and blood in action."

5. Suçruta.

(Calcutta Ed., p. 250; cf. Windisch in Sächs. Gesell. der Wiss., 1891, p. 193.)

(1) *Prāṇa* is the breath which goes in and out of the mouth, aids in swallowing the food, and is closely identified with life.

(2) *Udāna* is the breath which ascends upwards and upon which speech and singing depend.

(3) *Samāna* is the breath which functions in digestion.

(4) *Vyāna* is the breath which pervades the whole body and sets the fluids, the sweat and the blood, in motion.

(5) *Apāna* is the breath which takes the digested food and makes it into the excrement and semen; cf. Āit. Up. i. 3.

6. Buddhist Terminology.

(Cf. Kern's Manual of Buddhism, p. 65, in the Grundriss der Indo-Arischen Philologie.)

The terminology of Buddhists in the matter of breath control is significant. *Anāpānāu* takes the place of *prāṇāpānāu.*

One of the important so-called "spiritual" exercises bears the name *anāpānasmṛti.* It is absolutely certain that the generic term *ana* could not have been applied to the non-vital act of "out-breathing," and, therefore, *apāna* must have been so applied. On the other hand, it would not be impossible to include both in- and out-breathing under *ana,* in which case *apāna* would refer to the breath movements below the centre of the body.

"The Science of Breath."

In a recent book (1890) by Rāma Prasād, M.A., published by the Theosophical Society, which bears the title "Nature's Finer Forces," a Sanskrit treatise is translated under the caption "The

Science of Breath." The definitions of the members of the Prāṇa-Series are as follows:

(1) The Prāṇa lives always in the chest.
(2) The Apāna is in the circle of the anus.
(3) The Samāna is in the circle of the navel.
(4) The Udāna is in the midst of the throat.
(5) The Vyāna pervades the whole body.

The five other "winds" mentioned in the Vedāntasāra are also dealt with, the definitions thereof differing slightly from the Vedāntasāra.

The author calls attention to the fact that the Yogins, to which school the treatise belongs, make the navel the starting-point of the system of veins (*nāḍīs*) as against the Vedāntins who start from the heart. Further, much is made of the remarkable physiological (i. e. psychological) fact, based upon careful observation, that in breathing through the nose sometimes one nostril and sometimes the other is wholly used; sometimes one predominates and sometimes the other; while sometimes the flow of breath is as strong in one as in the other.

These variations are said to cause variations in psychical conditions.

VITA.

Arthur Henry Ewing was born at Saltsburg, Indiana County, Pa., October 18th, 1864; received his College preparatory education at Saltsburg and Elder's Ridge Academies; graduated from Washington and Jefferson College, Washington, Pa., in 1887, and from the Western Theological Seminary, Allegheny City, Pa., in 1890; sailed for India as a missionary in connection with the Presbyterian Church in September, 1890; was stationed at Ludhiana, Punjab, where he remained eight years engaged in educational, literary, and general work; returned to America in February, 1899, and spent two years as a resident graduate student in Johns Hopkins University, Baltimore, Md.

His principal subject, under the guidance of Professor Bloomfield, was Sanskrit. His subsidiary subjects were Philosophy and Arabic, under the guidance of Professors Griffin and Haupt.

He returned to India in February, 1901, to be stationed at Allahabad with a view to special educational work.